EPICUS
DOOMICUS
METALLICUS

PENTAGRAM

HELLRAISERS

Brimming with creative inspiration, how-to projects, and useful information to enrich your everyday life, Quarto Knows is a favorite destination for those pursuing their interests and passions. Visit our site and dig deeper with our books into your area of interest: Quarto Creates, Quarto Cooks, Quarto Homes, Quarto Lives, Quarto Drives, Quarto Explores, Quarto Gifts, or Quarto Kids.

Text © 2017 by Matthew Goldenberg and Christopher Krovatin
Cover image © 2017 by Mark Riddick / Riddickart

See page 286 for a complete listing of photo credits

First published in 2017 by Race Point Publishing, an imprint of The Quarto Group,
142 West 36th Street, 4th Floor, New York, NY 10018, USA
T (212) 779-4972 **F** (212) 779-6058 **www.QuartoKnows.com**

Race Point titles are also available at discount for retail, wholesale, promotional, and bulk purchase. For details, contact the Special Sales Manager by email at specialsales@quarto.com or by mail at The Quarto Group, Attn: Special Sales Manager, 401 Second Avenue North, Suite 310, Minneapolis, MN 55401, USA.

10 9 8 7 6 5 4 3 2

ISBN: 978-1-63106-430-2

Library of Congress Cataloging-in-Publication Data

Names: Rosenberg, Axl, 1982- author. | Krovatin, Christopher author.
Title: Hellraisers : a complete visual history of heavy metal mayhem / Axl
 Rosenberg and Christopher Krovatin.
Description: New York : Race Point Publishing, 2017. | Includes index.
Identifiers: LCCN 2017018379 | ISBN 9781631064302 (hardcover)
Subjects: LCSH: Heavy metal (Music)--History and criticism.
Classification: LCC ML3534 .R684 2017 | DDC 781.66--dc23
LC record available at https://lccn.loc.gov/2017018379

Editorial Director: Jeannine Dillon
Project Editor: Jason Chappell
Managing Editor: Erin Canning
Cover Image: Mark Riddick
Cover Design: Phil Buchanan
Interior Design: Jon Chaiet

Printed in China

HELLRAISERS

A COMPLETE VISUAL HISTORY OF HEAVY METAL MAYHEM

Axl Rosenberg and Christopher Krovatin

Race Point
PUBLISHING

This book is dedicated to the Birmingham
sheet-metal machine that ripped off
two of Tony Iommi's fingers.

Thanks for everything.

Contents

Matt Heafy, guitarist and vocalist for Trivium, and the dreamiest man in metal.

Foreword

Matt Heafy

Metal is not just a genre—it's a lifestyle. I have carried that idea with me since I first fell in love with metal. The first metal record I owned was *The Black Album* by Metallica. When I heard the music coming out of the speakers, I knew this was the music I was meant to live for. Inspired, I began tirelessly practicing guitar. Within a year of playing my eighth-grade talent show, I was asked to try out for a local high school metal band called Trivium. The rest is history.

A key element to being "metal" is knowing the genre's origins and the ever-evolving subgenres that spawn and multiply. Some roll their eyes at the dissections and microcosms of metal, but I have always loved that about the genre I call home. Metal is a wormhole—an endless spring of information and inspiration. After getting into Metallica, Pantera, Megadeth, and Slayer, I wanted more. I dug deeper into the realms of what else there could be. When I began my journey delving into the hellacious layers of underground metal, it was the era of Napster and metal magazines. I scoured the Internet and local music stores to find who else I might like. On Napster chat, I remember someone sending me what they called "melodic death metal."

The term sounded ear-catching, so I dug in. When I first heard "Jotun" by In Flames, my life was forever changed; I wanted to know what else there was like *this*.

I remember being in high school and explaining to friends who were just beginning to scratch the surface of heavy music what "melodic death metal" was. I would become filled with wonder and inspiration whenever discussing the Gothenburg sound, and how melodic death metal was the combination of mostly NWOBHM, death metal (from Stockholm, Sweden, and Tampa, Florida), and Swedish traditional folk music. I burned mixtape CDs for friends to bring them up to speed with the subgenres I loved so dearly: black metal, melodic death metal, and death metal. I still get excited when I can guess the country a band is from after hearing just a few seconds of their music.

I am so happy there is finally a book that explains metal the right way: in both scathing seriousness and comedic chaos.

Within the chapters of *Hellraisers*, you'll find both history and hilarity, along with starter kits of a subgenre and homework to listen to. Axl Rosenberg and Christoper Krovatin are about to school your ass in all things Metal.

—Matthew K. Heafy

Introduction

Good evening, students, and welcome to *Hellraisers*. We are Professors Rosenberg and Krovatin, and this semester, we'll be taking you on a trip through the history and culture of the single greatest musical innovation since a caveman began beating two femurs together in a 4/4 rhythm.

We are talking, of course, about Heavy Metal.

For those of you new to the world of extreme music, this course will be a primer/survey in heavy metal and all of its many niches. For those of you who are already knowledgeable about the genre, this course will be a refresher. Regardless of your prior experience, this course will entertain you and provoke thought, because we both have tenure, and can therefore say pretty much whatever we want up here. Some of our opinions may be unpopular, but remember: you already paid the fee up front.

So with all that shit out of the way, let's begin. First of all: What is metal?

The easy answer is that metal is a form of rock 'n' roll with everything turned up to eleven.

The hard answer is there is no easy answer. To declare "I love metal" is a bit like saying "I love comedy"—just as there are many different styles of comedy, there are many different styles of metal.

The truth is, metal's an ethos, a style, a state of mind. It's a spiritual path in which overkill is the primary virtue. It's a self-sustaining ecosystem of big personalities, extreme sounds, and stupid fucking outfits that keeps evolving into larger, scarier life forms.

Let's dive in with some basic, irrefutable truths, shall we?

1. **METAL IS AWESOME.** Search your feelings. You know it to be true.
2. **METAL IS FOR EVERYONE.** It is a fan's record collection and tattoo choices that make him or her a poseur, not where they're from, what they look like, the god they worship, or the people they bang (or don't worship, or don't bang). Nazi punks fuck off.
3. **METAL CAN BE FUNNY.** Yes, even if you love it. As the old saying goes, if you can't laugh at yourself, you're probably a Nickelback fan.
4. **JUST BECAUSE SOMETHING'S AWESOME DOESN'T MEAN IT'S METAL.** You're allowed to like Lady Gaga, but don't give us your diatribe about how she's more metal than Judas Priest. It's possible to be cool without being metal, just as it's possible (unfortunately) to be metal without being cool. Do not conflate the two.
5. **LISTEN TO METAL ABOVE ALL ELSE.** At the end of the day, metal is all about the music. So even if you don't wear spiked leather, or you like the color pink, or you've never heard of Celtic Frost, it doesn't mean you can't enjoy metal. Put some metal on right now and rock the fuck out!

About This Book

Now that we've covered the basics, we'll begin our syllabus of metal's long and storied history. The major chapters of this book cover different genres of metal. These lessons will begin with some basic information about that genre and conclude with a "homework assignment" playlist highlighting some of the genre's finest artists and songs. We'll also include a Starter Pack guide—the basic items you'll need if you want to take part in a metal subculture. Each chapter starts this way:

WHAT IS IT? A description of what this genre sounds like.

WHO LISTENS TO IT? A profile of the average fan of this kind of metal.

WHERE DOES IT COME FROM? The parts of the world from which this type of metal rushes forth.

BASTARD CHILDREN: Metal is a stratified style—every genre has subgenres, and those subgenres have subgenres of their own. Here, we'll try to amass each genre's many offspring.

THE BIG FOUR[1]: The top four bands in this genre. Consider them the bands you should know for the test.

Finally, we'd like to remind you that a LOT has happened in the fifty-year history of heavy metal, and there have been a LOT of really great bands. Alas, we only have a semester to cover all of this, so we'll just have time to acknowledge the heaviest hitters. If/when you come across a genre you enjoy, we strongly encourage you to continue your education on your own. There is an entire world of incredible music out there just waiting to sully your ears.

Got all that? Good. Ready? Tough shit. We're starting anyway.

---

1 Your first fun fact: The Big Four was a group of four thrash bands that dominated the metal scene in the 1980s (see Thrash, p. 95). The Big Four of Thrash are Metallica, Slayer, Megadeth, and Anthrax.

Proto-Metal

(Or, Metal Before It Was Called Metal)

WHAT IS IT?

Brusque and bluesy classic rock on drugs.

WHO LISTENS TO IT?

Everyone when they're thirteen.

WHERE DOES IT COME FROM?

Industrial Britain, heartland America, Australia.

BASTARD CHILDREN:

Heavy metal, hard rock, heavy rock, heavy blues, early punk, classic metal.

THE BIG FOUR:

Led Zeppelin, Alice Cooper, AC/DC, Black Sabbath.

Since the Middle Ages, humanity has been disturbed by the tritone. A musical interval comprised of three whole tones, the tritone is dissonant and restless, begging for another chord to support it and forcing the listener to anticipate another chord that may never come. The human ear naturally craves symmetry and resolution; music lacking these attributes inspires fear, anxiety, confusion, and rage.

Like all interesting art, the tritone was labeled evil. Its pointed dissonance earned it the title *diabolus in musica*, or "the Devil in music." Rumors that musicians were excommunicated from the church for performing the interval are probably just fables. The more believable story is that Vatican officials listed the tritone as potentially dangerous—meaning it made people want to have sex—and made a point of not using it in ecclesiastical music.

What makes the vilification of the tritone interesting is that such a dissonant musical tone is somehow attractive to listeners. This implies that people want to experience darkness, to indulge in the excitement and energy of anger, sorrow, and sin.

Throughout history, classical composers like Claude Debussy and Franz Liszt have used the tritone to add weight and power to their music. But the man who finally opened wide the gates of the abyss wasn't a European wig-wearer. He was a black dude from Seattle named Jimi.

HIPPIES WHO LIKE LEATHER

Former hippies would have you believe that the "Love Generation" washed away the drab normality of the 1950s in a tidal wave of tambourine and embroidery. This is revisionist history. The revolution's birth was a painful one, and the confusion and disillusionment that it caused was funneled directly into the music of the time.

Rock 'n' roll's intensity and agony was always present in America's black communities. Delta bluesmen and New York jazz savants were inspired by the cultural and economic woes experienced daily in black America, and used music to express and escape their pain. For white listeners, the fact that this complicated, enthralling music was made by the ultimate Other led them to create myths and superstitions surrounding it. One of the favorites is that Robert Johnson, the godfather of blues guitar, got his talent by making a deal with the Devil at a crossroads. To many, the story

Robert Johnson, godfather of the blues and purported business partner of Lucifer.

made sense—something so wonderful and yet so painful as Johnson's music had to be put on this earth by Satan himself.

It's hard to believe Old Scratch was controlling Elvis Presley, Jerry Lee Lewis, and the Beatles, whose perfectly tailored outfits and personas seemed less than satanic. But the moral authorities of the time were quick to invent the wickedness they sought to find in rock music. Elvis swinging his hips? A declaration that he wanted to thrust his pelvis into wholesome teenage girls. Paul McCartney asking a girl for her hand? Obviously, he planned to place that hand on his writhing groin. Jerry Lee Lewis singing about great balls of fire? The fire is hellfire, and the balls—well, you get the idea.

Of these bands, the Beatles were the ones who turned out to be the most "dangerous," their carefully managed personas hiding four good ol' boys who just wanted to make bank and meet chicks. In his autobiography, *White Line Fever*, Motörhead frontman and lifelong Beatles fan Lemmy Kilmister explains:

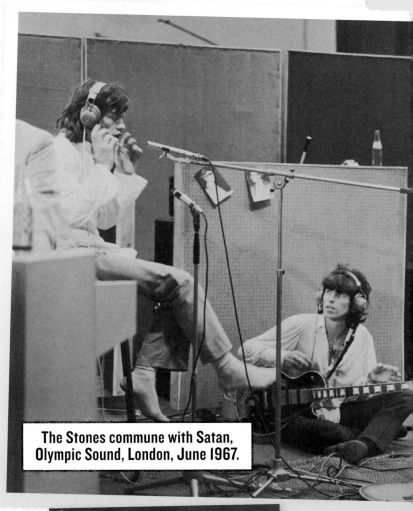

The Stones commune with Satan, Olympic Sound, London, June 1967.

> "The Beatles were hard men . . . they were from Liverpool, which is like Hamburg or Norfolk, Virginia—a hard, sea-farin' town, all these dockers and sailors all around that'd beat the piss out of you if you so much as winked at them. Ringo's from the Dingle, which is like the fucking Bronx. The Rolling Stones were the mummy's boys—they were all college students from the outskirts of London. They went to starve themselves in London, but it was by choice, to give themselves some sort of aura of disrespectability."

Jimi Hendrix performs in 1968. If you don't like Jimi Hendrix, you suck.

To be fair, the Rolling Stones were vital to heavy metal's development with their chemically impaired dabbling in black magic. They also coined the persona of the Mule-Faced Sex Gypsy, a rugged biker hippie so ugly he was irresistible; this archetype was the backbone of the appeal of bands like Guns N' Roses and Poison (see Glam Metal, page 63). But while Mick Jagger sang about sympathizing with Satan, Lennon and McCartney possessed a more subconscious menace. Their jauntiest tune is about a medical student beating women to death with a silver hammer. After luring

in the fanatic teenage daughters of the world, they started smoking weed, going to India, and trading their pop-star trappings for psychedelia and soul, in a natural reaction to the world crumbling around them.

No cultural event inspired the birth of heavy metal more than the Vietnam War. The carnage that 'Nam introduced to the average person—children murdered, forests napalmed, GIs wearing necklaces of ears—crushed any remaining normalcy and sexual repression left over from the 1950s. This spawned a generation of driven,

progressive revolutionaries who wanted to expand their minds and fight the power. But it also birthed a new breed of misanthropic stoners who wanted to drown out the massive letdown of witnessing humanity's true nature in a flood of electric guitar.

The last of the great hippie musicians was Jimi Hendrix, a ragged-haired African-American frontman who dressed like a colorblind pirate and moaned soulful lyrics about fire, voodoo, and Joe shooting his wife. He was also a brilliant guitarist who could make his ax exude both ass-shaking melodies and roaring waves of noise. His death

in 1970 was prophetic—one last bad vibe for a generation that was wondering if all vibes were bad at the end of the day.

Of his many awesome songs, Hendrix is most remembered for "Purple Haze," the opener of 1967's *Are You Experienced.* The song is known for its catchy central riff and an often-misheard line in its chorus. But for the rock and roll mythologist, the eight accents of crunching guitar that open the track are most important. That dissonant tone is the diminished fifth—the Devil's tritone. With it, Hendrix uncorked the bottle containing all the evils of rock and roll, and unleashed them onto the world.

The Zep holding the *Zeppelin II* master tapes at Honolulu Airport, May 12, 1969.

MUSIC TO TAKE
YOUR SHIRT OFF TO

The etymology of the term "heavy metal" isn't entirely clear. The periodic table of elements contains several heavy metals, including highly radioactive uranium. In his novel *The Soft Machine*, author and drug enthusiast William S. Burroughs includes a character named "Uranium Willy, the Heavy Metal Kid"; Burroughs would go on to use the term for hard drugs. Weirdo art collective Hapshash and the Coloured Coat named their 1967 album *With the Human Collective and the Heavy Metal Kids*. For most fans, though, the name comes from Steppenwolf's 1968 single "Born to Be Wild," which includes the line, "I like smoke

and lightning / Heavy metal thunder!" The song's use of the term and its outlaw sensibilities officially designated "heavy metal" as the title for a specific brand of muscular rock.

But metal's early forefathers didn't particularly like the title, and whether or not their music qualifies as metal has long been debated over six or more beers. Some bands, like Michigan's MC5 or Iggy Pop and the Stooges, possessed tons of raw energy but not enough low end and grind. Others, like British fantasy-rock group Jethro Tull and Long Island heavy soul band Vanilla Fudge, had plenty of groove but not enough fire.

The best example of a band that was metal but not really metal is Led Zeppelin. Why Led Zeppelin is not a metal band isn't exactly clear—it has all the pieces of a metal band, including a powerful rhythm section, a brilliant guitarist, and a sexually unhinged singer shrieking about hobbits—but it's widely accepted that, though it influenced metal in a number of ways, Led Zeppelin itself is not metal.

Part of this might be that Led Zeppelin is too universal for one subgenre. By the time they stopped calling themselves the New Yardbirds, Jimmy Page (guitar), Robert Plant (vocals), John Paul Jones (bass), and John Bonham (drums) were already on their way to being the biggest band in the world—a title they held throughout the 1970s as they toured in a private plane and banged every up-and-coming model they could. Their music actively courts mainstream enjoyment, never fully committing to metal's misanthropic melodrama. Page wrote dark, forceful riffs ("Immigrant Song" and "Kashmir"), but he also wrote an eight-minute, nonsensical ballad that became the most requested FM radio song of all time ("Stairway to Heaven").

That said, Zeppelin's influence on heavy metal is undeniable. Jimmy Page's riffs are dire, vital, and catchy as hell. The band's mythic destruction of hotel rooms fed the concept of the rock star as unhinged lord of the universe. Page's buying of the Scottish home of fabled occultist Aleister Crowley and the band's use of symbols instead of a title for its fourth album is the stuff of black metal daydreams. The Led Zeppelin hermit poster is the international symbol for basement marijuana consumption.

Even at Zeppelin's strongest, however, Page's guitar licks make heads bob rather than truly bang. For riffs with blunt force impact, fans had to turn to Australia's AC/DC.

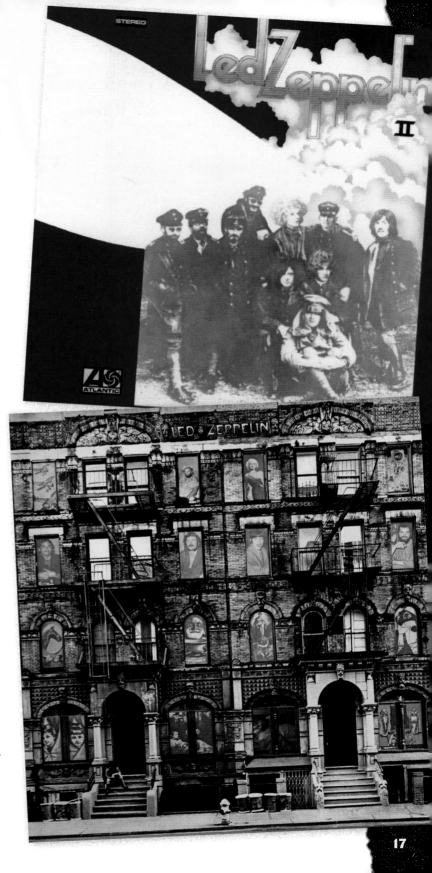

AC/DC's Angus Young dicking around, London, August 1979.

If all the drunk, horny people in the world threw a party, AC/DC would be the soundtrack. Everyone knows at least one AC/DC song. You yourself are softly singing an AC/DC song in your head right now, as you read this. Which one? "Back in Black"? "Highway to Hell"? Here, write it down in the space provided:

AC/DC Song I'm Rocking Out To in My Head:

It's a tale as old as time: two guitar-playing brothers, Malcolm and Angus Young, got together to make a lot of high-energy noise. After going through a couple of lineup changes, they settled on bassist Cliff Williams, drummer Phil Rudd, and hard-drinking vocalist Bon Scott. Angus began performing in costume, finally choosing a schoolboy uniform. The band played hopped-up electric blues about getting wasted and laid, and all the rockers and speed freaks got super into it, elevating AC/DC to international fame. After several kickass releases, they dropped *Back in Black*, an album that everyone wants to hear while they're drunk, and which eventually became the second-highest-selling record of all time (before you ask, *Thriller* by Michael Jackson is number one). Perhaps, like Led Zeppelin, this is why it's widely accepted that AC/DC is not a metal band—it's just too much fun for everyone.

Everyone, that is, but AC/DC, whose career reads like a bad rap sheet. In 1980, Scott choked to death on his own vomit. The band continued on with singer Brian Johnson, whose shriek was more stylized than Scott's. Then, in 1985, Los Angeles serial killer Richard "Night Stalker" Ramirez left an AC/DC cap at the scene of one of his murders,

prompting the media to take the band's fun-loving lyrics about road trips to Hades way too seriously. The track "Night Prowler," from 1979's *Highway to Hell*, was implicated, its eerie, imaginative lyrics making it believable as poetry that could send a broken mind into frenzy ("As you lay there naked, like a body in a tomb / Suspended animation as I slip into your room"). The band was caught up in the "Satanic Panic" of the 1980s, when heavy metal's diabolical influence on teenagers became the subject of every daytime talk show.

Sadly, trouble continues to follow AC/DC. The band has lost four of its heavyweights: Malcolm Young (dementia), Cliff Williams (retired), Phil Rudd (trying to hire a hit man), and Brian Johnson (hearing loss). Johnson was replaced with none other than Guns N' Roses frontman Axl Rose (see Glam Metal, page 63). While some were excited by AXL/DC, others weren't; in 2016, over seven thousand Belgian fans asked to have their tickets refunded upon discovering that Rose would be singing for them.

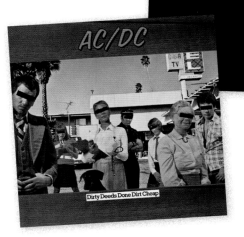

Charlie Manson gets his comeuppance, 1969. He was booked under the name "Manson, Charles M., aka Jesus Christ, God." Seriously.

IF IT BLEEDS, IT LEADS

While the hippie generation elicited little more than amusement and frumpy disdain during its rise to mainstream recognition, everything changed in 1969, when four hippies brutally murdered five people at the Los Angeles home of actress Sharon Tate and director Roman Polanski. The assailants were members of the "Family" of megalomaniacal charlatan Charlie Manson, who had fed them copious amounts of LSD, convinced them he was both God and the Devil, and turned them into a brainwashed cult of psychopath love children.

The Manson Family proved all the wrong people right, publicly illustrating that the acid-rocker's true agenda was murder in the name of feeling groovy. Manson had been an aspiring singer-songwriter known to Dennis Wilson of the Beach Boys; now, suddenly a song like "Good Vibrations" could be seen as the ecstasy of a killer. Slowly, bands picked up on the media wildfire surrounding the case, realizing that if it could sell newspapers, it could sell records. The result was shock rock—loud-ass theatrical rock music accompanied by costumes, fireworks, and maybe some fake blood.

Shock rock is blue collar by nature; if you spend your hard-earned money on a ticket, you deserve a fucking show. (A similar appeal applies to monster truck rallies.) Among the genre's early pioneers was Arthur Brown, who would wear a flaming helmet while performing "Fire," his namesake band's hit single, which is best known for the opening line, "I am the god of hellfire!" Brown is also known for influencing face painting in metal, a practice that has become grimly serious since the advent of corpse paint (see Black Metal, page 149). That said, Brown was nothing compared to KISS, whose effects-filled concerts and stylized face-paint designs truly inspired early black metal's live performances.

But the king of shock was Alice Cooper from Detroit. Cooper is to KISS as the Addams Family is to the Munsters; while the latter is made up of familiar terrors wearing big smiles, the former is simply an elegant maniac, an all-purpose dastardly character who might have worked in a circus.

Young fans who grew up on pornogrind (see Death Metal and Grindcore, page 123) will no doubt find Alice Cooper kind of lame. The darkness in his music always takes the form of boyish mischief, which is epitomized in the 1972 hit "School's Out" (you know the chorus). 1975's *Welcome to My Nightmare*, the first album Cooper made after officially adopting the name as a solo artist, contains straightforward horror, but even then its songs about giant spiders ("The Black Widow"), cannibalism ("Devil's Food"), necrophilia ("Cold Ethyl"), and murdering your wife ("The Awakening") are all spooky rather than brutal.[1] Even when it included straitjackets, line-dancing skeletons, and the infamous guillotine act, Alice Cooper's live horror show was more show than horror, and musically he was catchy and cinematic, with sweeping piano alongside chugging guitars. The "shock" in question wasn't, say, the alarming grotesquery of Cannibal Corpse.

At the time, though, people were freaked the fuck out. The band's back-alley transvestite style got it signed to Straight Records, owned by rock surrealist Frank Zappa. Things came to a perfect

---

[1] The record also contains the heartfelt anti–domestic violence ballad "Only Women Bleed," suggesting that while Alice was happy to bang dead women, he did not support beating live ones.

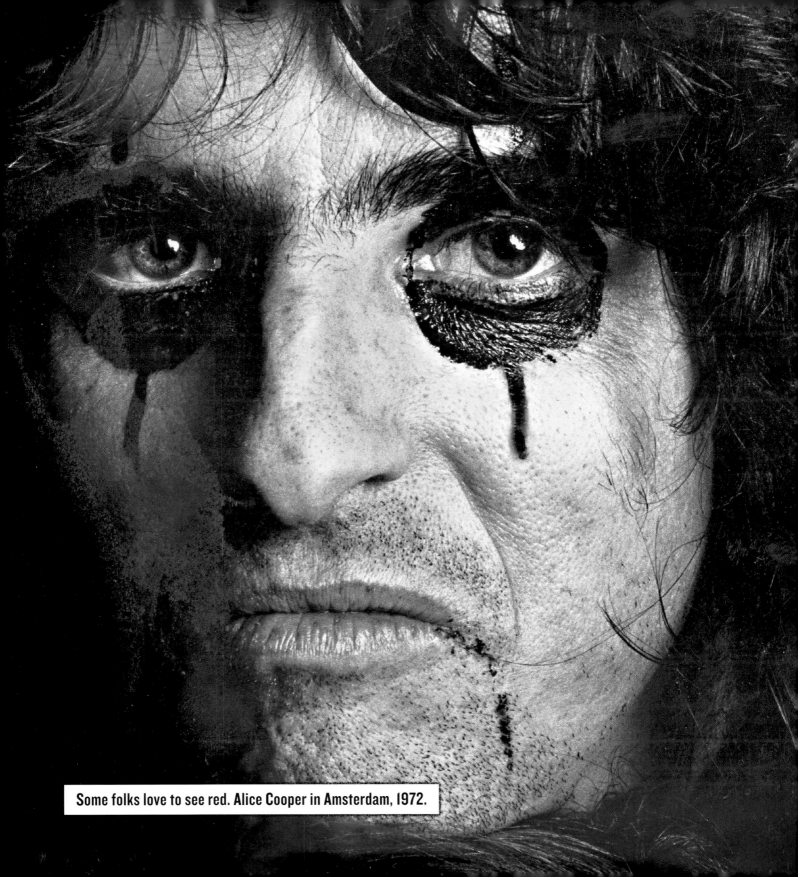

Some folks love to see red. Alice Cooper in Amsterdam, 1972.

head at the Toronto Rock and Revival fest in 1969, when a chicken was placed onstage during Alice Cooper's set. Cooper, assuming all birds could fly, released the chicken into the air; it sank like a stone, and the crowd tore it to shreds. He describes a phone call with Zappa about the incident in his episode of VH1's *Behind the Music*:

> **So I get a call from Zappa, saying, "Did you kill a chicken onstage?"**
> **And I said, "No!"**
> **And he said, "Well, don't tell anybody that! Everybody loves it! You're the most notorious character of all time now!"**

Alice Cooper's music wasn't initially metal— *Welcome to My Nightmare* sounds more like Meat Loaf than Maiden—but as the genre evolved, he went with the flow. From 1986's *Constrictor* onward, his music aped that of the edgier glam bands of the time, incorporating big choruses, melodramatic keyboards, and party-along lyrics. This culminated with 1991's *Hey Stoopid*, which features "Feed My Frankenstein," a horror-themed sex anthem made popular for appearing in *Wayne's World* shortly before Wayne and Garth kowtow before Cooper, screaming, "WE'RE NOT WORTHY!"

Alice then went on to embrace influences from genres like alternative (1994's *The Last Temptation* came out alongside a comic book written by *American Gods* author Neil Gaiman) and nu metal (2000's *Brutal Planet*, which shares its name with a popular haunted-house attraction). Thanks to him, musicians like GG Allin, GWAR, Ghoul, and Slipknot knew to get the crowd interested by doing some utterly insane shit onstage.

We're not worthy! Alice Cooper in Germany, late '70s.

GROUND ZERO BIRMINGHAM

So Led Zeppelin was metal lyrically, Alice Cooper was metal thematically, and AC/DC was metal spiritually. But at the end of the day, metal, like all good things, required a blood sacrifice to be properly born.

At the age of seventeen, British guitarist Tony Iommi lost the tips of the middle and ring fingers on his right hand in an accident at the sheet-metal factory where he worked. After being told he'd never play guitar again, he decided to go for it anyway and built himself a homemade prosthetic out of strips of leather from an old jacket and thimbles. Because he couldn't feel the strings, Iommi would strike them harder than necessary, and he began tuning his guitar down so he could better bend them. These factors added up to a guitar sound reminiscent of steel gears grinding against each other in a madman's dream.

After breaking up their previous band, Mythology, Iommi and drummer Bill Ward responded to an ad in the paper and met up with singer John "Ozzy" Osbourne, who then brought on bassist Geezer Butler. They called their band Earth, but after being mistaken for another band named Earth, they decided to ditch the moniker. The cinema across from their rehearsal space was showing the 1963 Boris Karloff movie *Black Sabbath*, so they went with that, and wrote a slow, creeping song about a satanic black mass.

The song, "Black Sabbath," opens with three dark, ominous tones—the Devil's tritone, spoken in the throaty growl of Iommi's guitar. With that, Black Sabbath became the first heavy metal band. Their first five records—1970's self-titled debut, '70's *Paranoid*, '71's *Master of Reality*, '72's *Vol. 4*, and '73's *Sabbath Bloody Sabbath*—are the bones on which the entire body of metal music was formed.

Ozzy fucking Osbourne in Oklahoma, 1976.

While Iommi's guitar sound is what sets Black Sabbath apart from its contemporaries, it is undeniably Ozzy Osbourne who gives the band its apocalyptic allure. On paper, Osbourne is not a terrific frontman, with his onstage tendency to clap and smile like a disturbed child. He also spent much of his career being famously unreliable, due to his love of drugs and alcohol. But the guy is credible by reason of insanity. His reedy cries about death and the Devil swallowing the world are upsettingly genuine and smack of the Manson Family's drug-soaked madness.

Like all great bands of the time, Black Sabbath's initial success gave way to mediocre albums and too many drugs. Osbourne's erratic, cocaine-fueled behavior led to his being fired in 1979 (the same year he married his eventual manager, Sharon). He was replaced by Ronnie James Dio, a diminutive American singer with a

Hell yes, we smoke marijuana in Muskogee! Black Sabbath play Oklahoma, 1976.

booming operatic voice, at which point the band's sound transformed into what we now think of as traditional metal, full of bright distortion, galloping rhythms, and a small singer wailing away up front. They released two solid records, 1980's *Heaven and Hell* and 1981's *Mob Rules*, before Dio left to start a solo career. After a semi-decent album featuring Deep Purple's Ian Gillian, 1983's *Born Again*, the band's output became a little tired and typical.

By the late 1990s, Ozzy Osbourne had cornered the market on mainstream metal. He and Sharon were running Ozzfest, a traveling metal festival featuring all the biggest names in angry-white-kid music. Bands like System of a Down, Slipknot, and Dimmu Borgir launched their careers by dominating Ozzfest's second stage. Meanwhile, in 1994, Sony released a Black Sabbath tribute album, *Nativity in Black*, which introduced the up-and-coming nu-metal generation to the band via covers by Faith No More, White Zombie, and Type O Negative.

Dio, circa 1970.

The Sabbath songbook.

In 1997, the original Sabbath lineup reunited to tour with Ozzfest and release a double live album, *Reunion*. The record was a huge hit: it went gold in the United States and finally won the band a Grammy in 2000 (for "Iron Man," some thirty years after it was originally released). In 2006, the band was inducted into the Rock and Roll Hall of Fame by none other than Metallica. The Dio-era lineup reunited as Heaven & Hell and put out 2009's *The Devil You Know*, the last album Dio would record before his unfortunate death from cancer in 2010.

Next came *13*, Sabbath's nineteenth studio release, which won the band another Grammy. The album was surrounded by controversy, as it claimed to reunite the "original lineup" of the band even though Bill Ward didn't play drums. Ward then came out publicly decrying Sabbath's business practices, claiming he was given a "totally unsatisfactory contract." Ozzy publicly fired back at Bill on Facebook, proving you're never too old to act like a dumb fucking teenager.

After *13*, Sabbath announced its farewell tour, "The End." The massive, multi-year trek concluded at a show in the band's hometown of Birmingham in 2017, thus bringing to a close the career of the first metal band. By the time you've read this, you'll most likely have bought your tickets to the reunion tour.

FROM HERE TO OBLIVION

At this point, whether metal had any idea what it was doing remained unclear. The bands that would be lumped into the category—English heavy-rockers Foghat, Scottish shriekers Nazareth, and Canadian progressive neo-pagans Rush—were nothing alike and had no musical loyalty to one another. Deep Purple wowed fans with its distinctive heavy riffs, including Beavis and Butthead sing-along "Smoke on the Water," and Blue Öyster Cult was known for its creepy autumnal ballad "Don't Fear the Reaper," but these were cases of metal being accidentally tripped over rather than played for the sake of playing it.

But though it was a hare-lipped bastard child wandering the musical wasteland with its pants down, heavy metal had been born. And though antisocial and misanthropic by nature, this fledgling genre harbored dreams of world domination. When the next generation of rock-and-rollers finally announced that they were looking for something bigger, crazier, and louder than anything else, heavy metal was ready to receive them with horns sharpened and muscles rippling.

Blue Öyster Cult spook out Tulsa,
Oklahoma, July 25, 1975.

Starter Kit

Ready to tune in, turn on, and drop
the fuck out? You will need:

- [ ] HAIR, 18 IN., UNWASHED, STRAIGHT OR PERMED

- [ ] ONE (1) DENIM JACKET, OPENED TO ONE'S BARE CHEST

- [ ] ONE (1) PAIR BELL-BOTTOMED JEANS, POCKETS EMBROIDERED

- [ ] ONE (1) BLACK LIGHT

- [ ] ONE (1) FRANK FRAZETTA POSTER TO HANG OVER THE AFOREMENTIONED BLACK LIGHT

- [ ] THREE (3) CAPSULES HIGH-GRADE MESCALINE

- [ ] ZAP! COMIX #2 POKING OUT OF YOUR BACK POCKET

- [ ] DREAMS, SHATTERED

- [ ] AP MATH CLASS IN AN HOUR

Homework

1. **THE JIMI HENDRIX EXPERIENCE, "PURPLE HAZE"**

   (Are You Experienced, 1967)

2. **CREAM, "SUNSHINE OF YOUR LOVE"**

   (Disraeli Gears, 1967)

3. **THE BEATLES, "COME TOGETHER"**

   (Abbey Road, 1969)

4. **THE ROLLING STONES, "SYMPATHY FOR THE DEVIL"**

   (Beggar's Banquet, 1968)

5. **THE CRAZY WORLD OF ARTHUR BROWN, "FIRE"**

   (The Crazy World of Arthur Brown, 1968)

6. **MC5, "KICK OUT THE JAMS"**

   (Kick Out the Jams, 1969)

7. **BLUE CHEER, "SUMMERTIME BLUES"**

   (Vincebus Eruptum, 1968)

8. **BLACK SABBATH, "BLACK SABBATH"**

   (Black Sabbath, 1970)

9. **LED ZEPPELIN, "IMMIGRANT SONG"**

   (Led Zeppelin II, 1970)

10. **AC/DC, "DIRTY DEEDS DONE DIRT CHEAP"**

    (Dirty Deeds Done Dirty Cheap, 1976)

11. **ALICE COOPER, "SCHOOL'S OUT"**

    (School's Out, 1972)

12. **MOUNTAIN, "MISSISSIPPI QUEEN"**

    (Climbing, 1970)

13. **DEEP PURPLE, "SMOKE ON THE WATER"**

    (Machine Head, 1972)

14. **BLACK SABBATH, "IRON MAN"**

    (Paranoid, 1970)

15. **THIN LIZZY, "EMERALD"**

    (Jailbreak, 1972)

16. **LED ZEPPELIN, "KASHMIR"**

    (Physical Graffiti, 1975)

17. **BLUE ÖYSTER CULT, "DON'T FEAR THE REAPER"**

    (Agents of Fortune, 1976)

18. **MEAT LOAF, "BAT OUT OF HELL"**

    (Bat Out of Hell, 1977)

19. **HAWKWIND, "MOTORHEAD"**

    ("King of Speed" single, 1975)

20. **BLACK SABBATH, "CHILDREN OF THE GRAVE"**

    (Master of Reality, 1971)

21. **ALICE COOPER, "STEVEN"**

    (Welcome to My Nightmare, 1975)

22. **AC/DC, "BACK IN BLACK"**

    (Back in Black, 1980)

Black Sabbath in the 1970s, before they toughened up.

Metal Bassists: Fewer Strings, Less Respect

Bassists take a lot of shit in metal. It's not entirely clear when this trend began (although it was surely sometime after the death of legendary Metallica bassist Cliff Burton, page 96), but it seems to be rooted largely in two facts: bass guitars usually have fewer strings than regular guitars and guitarists often record a band's bass lines in the studio.

But "bassists are the unsung heroes of metal," according to Nail the Mix's Eyal Levi, a producer, engineer, mixer, and educator who over the past fifteen years has worked with a myriad of popular modern metal bands, including Deicide, Whitechapel, and DevilDriver. "Since bass players generally don't play solos and the bass isn't a lead instrument, it hasn't been as attractive to certain types of musicians, who generally gravitate toward instruments that will get them attention, like the guitar. So bass gets overlooked a lot. And without it, you're fucked."

> "It's almost one of those things that's unteachable—either you've got it or you don't."

And why, pray tell, are you fucked without a good bassist? "Lots of people don't realize that a really great guitar tone on a metal record, a tone that's huge and has teeth and fills up

Cliff Burton blows the colon out of Des Moines, Iowa, 1986.

the room and tears your head off, isn't just guitars—it is, at least in part, a bass tone blended with guitars," Levi explains. "And it's not just the low end. The bass also contributes to the mids of the sound, and to how aggressive the drums sound. If you somehow get your hands on the multi-tracks for a song that's been really well mixed, try taking the bass out. You'll notice that suddenly all the life has been sucked out of the recording. Even though you can't always identify the bass in metal the way you can in, say, funk music, where there isn't a competing instrument, it's very important."

Nor, according to Levi, should anyone buy into the myth that it takes less work to become a great bassist than it does to become a great guitarist. "It's a different kind of discipline," he says. "To really be great at bass, you have to be technical enough to keep up, you have to play really hard but not too hard, and you need to understand rhythm in a way that's more relatable to drummers than guitarists—the bass is almost a hybrid of the guitar and the drum. You need to understand how to translate stuff on the fretboard into a feel that locks with the drummer. Bass adds this pocket to the music that no other instrument can add, and that's a very, very difficult thing to learn. It's almost one of those things that's unteachable—either you've got it or you don't."

Insofar as guitarists recording bass lines in the studio, Levi says it's a decision that has nothing to do with skill. "Two people cannot match feels exactly the same way. It's like with handwriting—everyone has their own unique feel. And one thing that's really important in metal is that you have a really huge guitar sound that drives the whole thing. Sometimes you get variations in the left and right guitar, but often left and right guitar are playing the same thing. One of the reasons that's effective as a driving force is because their timing is locked. If you take two guitars that are locked and put a bass that isn't locked under them, that will detract from the impact. So you have the guitar player record the bass parts, too, because only he has that feel and can make the guitars and the bass sync up perfectly."

Cliff again, Tulsa, Oklahoma, 1985. We miss you, dude.

The New Wave of British Heavy Metal

WHAT IS IT?

Operatic muscle rock full of tasty fills and guitar acrobatics, with lyrics about killing fictional creatures.

WHO LISTENS TO IT?

Working-class vest-wearers who say "man" a lot, ultra-underground metalheads who need something to relax to, Italian teenagers.

WHERE DOES IT COME FROM?

Great Britain, the Netherlands.

BASTARD CHILDREN:

Opera metal, speed metal, classical metal, power metal, vest metal.

THE BIG FOUR:

Iron Maiden, Judas Priest, Venom, Motörhead.

Judas Priest in Rockford, Illinois, July 28, 1978.

nd so, wielding the Devil's tritone like a flaming sword, Black Sabbath sliced open the depressive womb of the 1970s, yanked out the wriggling child within it, and held it aloft so that the crowd could hear it scream.

But metal wasn't metal—not yet. Though Sabbath's unique brand of what drummer Bill Ward called "downer rock" was revolutionizing how evil music could sound, it was still slow, simple, and broken up by interludes of piddling psychedelia. If this music was to leave its beery thumbprint on the face of the world, it needed to offer more than just stomping riffs for weary potheads. It needed excitement, insanity, and, most of all, technicality.

For many of its creators, the New Wave of British Heavy Metal (NWOBHM) began with the sole intent of forming a band that sounded like Sabbath and Deep Purple but faster and louder. But while Sabbath was expressing the drabness of everyday life in industrial England, the NWOBHM bands were escaping it. The sonic scope and much-lauded rock star antics of Led Zeppelin, David Bowie, and Queen had taught them that

Judas Priest in Tulsa, Oklahoma, circa 1978. Look at Halford in his sleeves!

there was a wide world out there full of soaring singers and gravity-defying outfits. At the same time, the dramatic playing of bands like Thin Lizzy and Van Halen instilled in young British headbangers a respect for the technical ecstasy of classical music—albeit one that was channeled through a hairy 1970s biker sneer.

Armed with drama, overkill, and machismo, the next generation of bands made their guitars louder, their drums faster, their vocals higher, and their worlds bigger. Their music was over-the-top enough to earn the sheer weight of heavy and the

gleaming razor's edge of metal.

The band that got together first turned out to be the one that raised the heavy metal flag the highest—and, interestingly enough, hailed from the same town as Black Sabbath. Formed in 1969 and named after a Bob Dylan song, Judas Priest started out as just another noise complaint in bellbottoms until the combination of guitarists K. K. Downing and Glenn Tipton, bassist Ian Hill, and piercing falsetto singer Rob Halford turned the band into a powerhouse that sounded like the hum of a hoverbike engine as it soared over the apocalypse.

Priest put out several albums of groundbreaking proto-metal until striking gold with 1980's *British Steel*, famous for its genre-defining single "Breaking the Law."

Judas Priest's music is unequivocal. It sounds like metal—literally, like crashing sheets of steel set to infectious melody. Tipton and Downing's concussive riffs and slicing harmonies were purposefully honed to dangerous perfection. Halford's vocals were a mixture of snotty battlefield snarl and cloud-parting Valkyrie cry as he told operatic tales about scoring with chicks (or so we thought at the time). The band's musical and lyrical theme is one and the same: power.

After *British Steel*, Judas Priest became the forward face of heavy metal, embodying all of its undeniable strengths and hilarious flaws. The members dressed in studded leather to the point where they looked like bondage bikers from Mars; Halford even rocked a cop hat and would ride his motorcycle across the stage during live shows.

The band's songs were epic and technical but often told stories of killer robots and horny vampires. Their videos were massive hits on MTV; the band responded by trying to write keyboard-heavy radio singles. Unlike their peers, however, the members of Priest managed to pull their heads out of their own asses quickly enough, and in 1990 they released *Painkiller*, as dramatic and traditional a metal album as the world had seen since thrash became everyone's extreme music du jour (see Thrash Metal, page 93).

Judas Priest also embodied another metal stereotype: the heavy metal band that encouraged its fans to kill themselves. In 1990, the band was involved in a civil action suit in which it was claimed that after hours of drinking, smoking weed, and listening to Priest's 1978 album *Stained Class*, Raymond Belknap (age eighteen) and James Vance (age twenty) were driven to commit suicide by subliminal messages hidden in Judas Priest's music. Even worse, while Belknap succeeded in killing himself, Vance failed; horribly deformed by his self-inflicted gunshot wound, he became an unsettling poster boy for heavy metal's supposedly dark intentions.

Like a similar 1984 suit against Ozzy Osbourne, in which the anti-suicide ballad "Suicide Solution" was blamed for a teen's death, the trial of Judas Priest became a witch-hunt full of fake experts and campfire-story lawyers. Priest eventually won the case when it was remembered that it made no sense for a band to kill off its paying customers. However, the trial and others like it inspired a million and one washed-up psychologists to suddenly proclaim themselves experts on the shadowy underbelly of heavy metal culture.

Following the Painkiller tour, Halford left the band and went on to form a punchy thrash group named Fight. Priest started up again, fronted by Tim "Ripper" Owens, a former singer in a Judas Priest cover band whose story would later be turned into the cancerous Mark Wahlberg vehicle *Rock Star.*

Then Halford came out as gay in 1998.

This was huge. In the late '90s, heavy metal was seen as a cultural dinosaur, in part because of its toxic hyper-masculinity. To have not just a major metal musician but the Metal God come out as gay immediately showed the world that homosexuality existed

even in (perhaps especially in) the most masculine of subcultures. (Hell, Halford didn't even have long hair, which had always been a point of metalhead emasculation by dumbass rednecks and closet-case hardcore kids.) Thankfully, the metal community responded with rare grace, publicly lauding Rob for his bravery and supporting his decision (see Sexuality in Metal, page 85). The band eventually fired Owens and reunited with Halford, and continues to kill it live to this day.

The father of suicide victim John McCollum, pictured with the record he claimed killed his son.

Halford at the "Don't Go" photo shoot in 1981.

Am I evil? Meh. Diamond Head, 1983.

SCREAM FOR ME, READER!

For many, the *sturm und drang* of Priest was a
gateway drug. All across England, bands were
mixing heavy riffs with large-form hard rock.
Ozzy Osbourne began his post-Sabbath career by
biting the head off of a dove while meeting with
record executives; his debut solo album included
the smash hit "Crazy Train," the official heavy
metal track of minivan dads everywhere. Power-
metallers Diamond Head (or perhaps cheesy
doom-metallers?) became known for looming
guitar sound and dark lyrics; "Am I Evil?" was an
anthem for all metalheads who preferred demons
to dungeons, including Metallica, whose cover
of the track remains the primary reason why
anyone cares about Diamond Head. Meanwhile, in
Sheffield, a group named Atomic Mass underwent
lineup and name changes and became Def
Leppard. The band went on to become a hair-metal
juggernaut and feature, improbably, the most
famous one-armed drummer of all time.

Of course, everyone sucked compared to Iron
Maiden. Then again, Maiden wasn't trying to
sound like Judas Priest. The group had its own
thing going—eventually, at least—and it changed
metal forever.

Even if, for some weird reason, you're reading
this book despite having never cared about metal,
there's a great chance you know what Iron Maiden's
logo looks like. Though Iron Maiden may not be
the biggest metal band in the world—that honor
falls to Metallica (see Thrash Metal, page 93)—it
is certainly the most iconic. Like Judas Priest, its
members never wanted to be anything more than
a heavy metal band; unlike Priest, they didn't feel
the need to wear that fact on their sleeves. The
band's technical talent and catchy hooks spoke for
themselves.

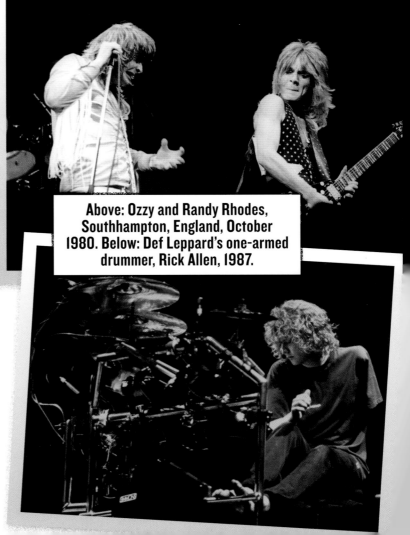

Above: Ozzy and Randy Rhodes, Southhampton, England, October 1980. Below: Def Leppard's one-armed drummer, Rick Allen, 1987.

The first two Iron Maiden albums, 1980's self-titled debut and 1981's *Killers*, are full of decent songs and showcase the beginnings of bassist Steve Harris's mind-blowing songwriting capabilities. For many old-school fans, including members of Slayer, they're important records. But singer Paul Di'Anno struggles with his harsh vocals in a way that makes it seem as though he's being outclassed by the band behind him. Mostly, these albums are notable for introducing the world to Eddie, Iron Maiden's leering zombie mascot (see Metal Mascots, page 59).

It was 1982's *The Number of the Beast* that put Maiden on the map. The album was the band's first to feature vocalist Bruce Dickinson, an intelligent and energetic frontman whose voice actually earns the often-overused adjective "soaring." Dickinson has a bombastic tenor wail with a mind-boggling range, and his indefatigable enthusiasm and puckish stage presence make him the frontman that a band as baroque and talented as Iron Maiden truly deserves. He also provided distinctly English lyrical themes—classic literature, East End harlots, and London during the Blitz—making Iron Maiden's underlying atmosphere synonymous with British metal.

With Dickinson on board, Iron Maiden became the band it was truly meant to be. Its music was too brilliant to be looked down on and too forceful to be yawned at. As big hair and glitter became the face of mainstream rock 'n' roll, Iron Maiden entertained sold-out festival crowds with tracks like "The Trooper" and "2 Minutes to Midnight," thus satisfying a generation of musicians who

Iron Maiden on the bus, September 1983. Woof, those shorts!

wanted a stiffer drink than the coconut rum cocktail of glam metal. Like every other great metal band, the group had some issues during the angst-choked 1990s, when Dickinson left and the band made two lousy albums about computers. But Maiden recovered quickly, with Dickinson returning in 2000 for the crushing *Brave New World*. The singer has since gotten his pilot's license and actually flies the band's touring plane, Ed Force One, thus making him the second-coolest frontman in all of metal (we have to do Venom first, and then we'll talk about #1).

Interestingly enough, Iron Maiden got hit with the satanic rap harder than its peers, even though the band barely mentioned the Devil at all. Sure, the cover of *Number* features Eddie using the Devil like a marionette as Lucifer himself uses a marionette of Eddie to entertain the hordes of hell (it's hard to explain; just look at the picture below, left). And, yes, the title track's lyrics have some demonic overtones (though "Six! Six six! The one for you and me!" is maybe the lamest thing any Satanist could say). But given that that track is Maiden's only real claim to devilry, the emphasis put on the band's involvement in the corruption of '80s youth was a little ridiculous. For years, TV preachers would hold up the sleeve of *Number* and point to the title as though it explained why some kids preferred smoking weed to doing homework.

Many other bands suffered somewhat foolishly through the Satanic Panic just as Maiden had. One such act was American power-metal group Dio, led by former Elf/Rainbow/Black Sabbath frontman Ronnie James Dio. Many metalheads learned the "Devil Horns" hand motion from Dio, but the singer

King Diamond of Mercyful Fate, 1983. He's going to put that inverted cross exactly where you think he will.

used it as the ancient sign to ward off the Evil Eye (he learned it from his Italian grandmother). Besides, all of Dio's songs were about being either a disillusioned teenager or some sort of valiant adventurer. Nonetheless, his music and logo were often displayed as a sign of devil worship that parents should look out for.

If you wanted Satan in the NWOBHM, the guys who were the most serious about it weren't even British: they were Danish. Mercyful Fate went full philosophical Satanism, primarily thanks to lead singer King Diamond, a Draculean character who accepted the nuanced fallen angel of Anton La Vey's Church of Satan as his lord and savior. Mercyful Fate was so unabashedly diabolic that one of its songs made it onto Tipper Gore's infamous "Filthy Fifteen" list (see Glam Metal, page 63). But even

the Fate's Satanism was tempered by the technical talent of its members. Diamond's explanations of his religion were always interesting and well spoken, never touching on virgin sacrifice or blood rites. And his vocals were delivered in an eardrum-shattering falsetto that, though eerie, sounded less than demonic to many metalheads.

For the less refined Satanist there was Venom, from Newcastle. If Mercyful Fate was a Hammer Horror movie—Victorian nobles in costumes talking about defiling the cross—Venom was a blood-drenched exploitation flick, complete with all the guts, bare breasts, and foul language that one would expect from a grindhouse double feature.

Venom is pretty much how most parents imagine heavy metal: loud, angry, sloppy, kind

a little too flowery and hackneyed to be truly tough; it was hard to be believably scary with vocal effects and keyboard solos. Venom, meanwhile, was influenced by punk and the emerging sounds of speed metal, and as such traded technicality for straight-up rage and grossness. The result is oddly compelling—buzz-saw guitar tones, steady drums, and snotty coughs about death and Satan. The emphasis on attitude over ability featured on fast-paced muggers like "Witching Hour" and pounding death marches like "Warhead" would heavily inform future thrash bands who could only take so many wheedling solos before they needed something with a bit more brawn.

Venom is also credited with spawning the many metal subgenre names that now dominate the scene. It was Cronos who—as he has brought up over and over again since—first used the term "black metal" to describe Venom; the band went on to make the phrase the title of its second full-length album. Meanwhile, its melodramatic and seemingly humorless style, including the use of demonic fake names, inspired death- and black-metal bands for decades to come.

of dumb, and super into Satan. Its albums had pentagrams or evil creatures wearing pentagrams on them, and if the band's songs weren't about hanging out with the Devil, they were about loose women (occasionally, they were about getting it on with loose women in front of the Devil, a topic that strangely appealed to a large number of metalheads). The guys in the band were called Cronos, Abaddon, and Mantas (Conrad, Anthony, and Jeffrey to their moms). They wore studded bondage gear and clutched skulls and bones in front of bonfires, cloaked in billows of fake smoke that hid their true intentions.

More than anything, Venom sounded evil, which was cool. For all of their killer riffs and sing-along hooks, most NWOBHM bands were

But no matter how rugged, fast, or angry it sounded, Venom was even cheesier than its peers. At least by not overdoing their evil personas, the members of Maiden and Priest didn't have to later admit that they were just some guys who liked having a beer now and then. Venom, meanwhile, was forced to concede that those satanic demeanors were a put-on, thus diminishing what made the band special to their fanbase.

WARTS AND ALL

Only one band could truly walk the walk and talk the talk. Like Venom, it didn't get too bogged down in technicality, but it also didn't need Halloween costumes to make the world stand back, mouths agape. Not with that frontman.

Ian Frasier Kilmister was born on Christmas Eve, 1945, in Stoke-on-Trent. As a schoolchild, Ian saw a classmate with a guitar "surrounded by chicks" and decided to bring his mother's guitar to school, long before he knew how to play it. At age sixteen, he saw the Beatles at the Cavern Club, and it inspired him to become a rock star. By age twenty-three, he was a roadie for Jimi Hendrix and being paid in hits of acid. His habit of borrowing money for the slot machines earned him the nickname Lemmy—as in, "Lemme borrow a fiver, mate."

Lemmy later joined space-rock crew Hawkwind as bassist and vocalist, but was fired from the band at the US/Canadian border for having a bunch of speed on him at the time. He decided that Hawkwind's indulgent psychedelic rock wasn't for him; instead, he was going to form a louder, meaner band that would play kick-ass rock 'n' roll songs about boozing, fucking, and feeling weird. Lemmy wanted to call the band Bastard, but he knew it couldn't get on Top of the Pops with a name like that, so he stole the title of the last song he wrote for Hawkwind and called the band Motörhead. With an umlaut. Because it looks cooler that way.

Motörhead's music is the soundtrack to a bar fight. Its songs are about whiskey, women, feeling down, listening to rock 'n' roll, and feeling better— all sung in a voice like a bad muffler on an old plane. Lemmy also had a distinct bass sound, trading the plunking tone of most bands for a growl of distortion and a riffy chug, so that every Motörhead song sounds as though there's a chopper's engine roaring in the background. Though the band released twenty-two albums with countless classics on them, it is 1980's *Ace of Spades* and its rip-roaring title track that will forever be remembered by fans, historians, and people who aren't metalheads attending a metal concert.

Even as a dude with no mug shot, Lemmy was still the ultimate rock 'n' roll outlaw. His hairy persona, radio-friendly looks, and steady and unabashed consumption of Jack Daniels and speed made him the ideal for any person who feels at home in black leather. While Ozzy was biting the head off of a dove, Lemmy was getting head onstage from a female fan. While Keith Richards was getting over heroin by having his blood cleaned, Lemmy was getting turned away at the door. From Kilmister's autobiography, *White Line Fever*:

> "I've got to tell you this," [the doctor] said. "Pure blood will kill you."
>
> "What?"
>
> "You don't have human blood any more. And you can't give blood, either. Forget it, you'd kill the average person because you're so toxic."

Shoot you in the back! Motörhead in London, 1978.

At the same time, Lemmy escaped cliché by being complicated and honest. The love of his life drowned in the bathtub while high on heroin, making a vocal enemy of smack out of the ultimate substance abuser. He wrote the ballad "Mama, I'm Coming Home" for Ozzy Osbourne and later claimed he made more money from that track than he did from Motörhead's many albums combined. He had a lifelong love of World War II paraphernalia that sometimes seemed questionable—Joe Petagno's original drawing of Snaggletooth, the Motörhead war pig (see Metal Mascots, 59), had a swastika on his helmet, which Lemmy later had removed—but he assured the world it was just a historical fascination.

Lemmy himself never considered Motörhead heavy metal—"Although we played it at a thousand miles an hour, it was recognizable as blues," he wrote, "at least it was to us; probably it wasn't to anyone else"—and the band's inclusion on this list will certainly be debated since much of Motörhead's early material was more like roughed-up garage rock than it was like Metallica. But Motörhead's later output—starting in the 1980s, after Lemmy lost all of his bandmates and had to reassemble the band from scratch—was distinctly metal, with just the right amount of glam's squealing guitar. More so, the no-frills honesty of the band's breakneck party rock would become a tenet of metal culture. When Lemmy sang about being born to lose, the losers listened, and they discovered that even if they were warty kids who only enjoyed getting in trouble, they too could have a good time without hurting anyone.

By the time Lemmy died (age seventy) of cancer in 2015, he was considered rock royalty, having never found Jesus, gotten sober, or accepted any of the other clichéd compromises that so many rock stars had scrambled for when the going got tough.

No sleep 'til Hammersmith

Read 'em and weep: the "Dead Man's Hand" again. A poker chip from the Motörboat Cruise.

Lemmy firing one off in 1978.

Take it like a band! Girlschool looking scary, hot, scarily hot, in 1983.

The cast of *Miami Vice*, wait, sorry, Saxon, in Chicago, August 1983.

AND LO, IT BECAME A THING

With Motörhead's punk-rock speed, the NWOBHM began to change. Plenty of bands, like the all-female Girlschool and the sports-obsessed Raven, began churning out heavy tunes full of straightforward rage that would be called "speed metal," a genre that sums up the growing pains between NWOBHM and thrash. Other bands created their own variations on Maiden's sound, including Saxon, whose "Denim and Leather" is a European metal anthem; Grim Reaper, which was pretty laughable in its D&D monster-manual interpretation of death and drama; and Witchfinder General, whose moody and gloomy music borrowed heavily from King Diamond's swooning Satanism.

More than that, the NWOBHM solidified the metalhead as a cultural trope—a specific type of rock fan whose fashion sense and attitude could be identified, quantified, and parodied. This is displayed in 1984's *This Is Spïnäl Tap*, a mockumentary following fictional heavy-metal forefathers Spïnäl Tap as their tour collapses and their band falls apart.

The film invented as many rock-star stereotypes as it mocked, from cranking your amps up to eleven to wandering the venue unable to find the stage. An actual documentary, 1986's *Heavy Metal Parking Lot*, takes a more anthropological approach by studying the drinking habits of a bunch of tailgaters at a Judas Priest concert.

For most metal bands, the mid-to-late '90s were a dire time; for the New Wave of British Heavy Metal, the glory days were already past by then. Those bands still making high-profile albums were going out on weird limbs and trying new things by 1990—even Maiden was using a lot of keyboards—and a new class of metal bands was blowing them out of the water with speedy, vicious interpretations of the classic NWOBHM sound. These bands had deeply absorbed Motörhead's message that it was okay to be ugly so long as you kicked ass, and they began pushing the boundaries of speed and good taste in the name of raw energy.

Before we get to them, though, let's talk about a bunch of assholes in lipstick.

Starter Kit

Ready to run to the hills and break
the law? You will need:

- [ ] HAIR, 8–10 IN.

- [ ] ONE (1) JACKET, DENIM OR LEATHER

- [ ] THREE-TO-FIVE (3–5) SMALL PATCHES FOR PLACEMENT AROUND JACKET

- [ ] ONE (1) LARGE BACK PATCH FOR THE BACK-CENTER OF THIS JACKET

- [ ] LIGHT BEER, 12–24 OZ.

- [ ] ONE (1) VAN SPRAY-PAINTED WITH THE ALBUM COVER OF YOUR CHOICE

- [ ] $12.52 FOR GASOLINE

- [ ] A CONFUSED CONCEPT OF MASCULINITY

Homework

Angel Witch

1. **JUDAS PRIEST, "BREAKING THE LAW"**

   (British Steel, 1980)

2. **DIAMOND HEAD, "AM I EVIL?"**

   (Lightning to the Nations, 1979)

3. **OZZY OSBOURNE, "CRAZY TRAIN"**

   (Blizzard of Ozz, 1980)

4. **ANGEL WITCH, "WHITE WITCH"**

   (Angel Witch, 1980)

5. **IRON MAIDEN, "RUN TO THE HILLS"**

   (The Number of the Beast, 1982)

6. **MOTÖRHEAD, "ACE OF SPADES"**

   (Ace of Spades, 1980)

7. **GIRLSCHOOL, "C'MON LET'S GO"**

   (Hit and Run, 1981)

8. **DEF LEPPARD, "HIGH AND DRY (SATURDAY NIGHT)"**

   (High 'n' Dry, 1981)

9. **VENOM, "IN LEAGUE WITH SATAN"**

   (Welcome to Hell, 1981)

10. **IRON MAIDEN, "THE TROOPER"**

    (Piece of Mind, 1983)

11. **SAXON, "DENIM AND LEATHER"**

    (Denim and Leather, 1981)

12. **JUDAS PRIEST, "YOU'VE GOT ANOTHER THING COMING"**

    (Screaming for Vengeance, 1982)

13. **IRON MAIDEN, "ACES HIGH"**

    (Powerslave, 1984)

14. **DIO, "DON'T TALK TO STRANGERS"**

    (Holy Diver, 1984)

15. **MOTÖRHEAD, "NO CLASS"**

    (No Sleep 'Til Hammersmith, 1982)

16. **WITCHFINDER GENERAL, "FREE COUNTRY"**

    (Witchfinder General, 1982)

17. **VENOM, "BLACK METAL"**

    (Black Metal, 1982)

18. **RAVEN, "MIND OVER METAL"**

    (All for One, 1983)

19. **GRIM REAPER, "FEAR NO EVIL"**

    (Fear No Evil, 1985)

20. **MERCYFUL FATE, "A DANGEROUS MEETING"**

    (Don't Break the Oath, 1984)

21. **IRON MAIDEN, "WASTED YEARS"**

    (Somewhere in Time, 1986)

Iron Maiden's Janick Gers gives Eddie the Head a piggyback ride, circa 2005.

Metal Mascots: Hell Anthropomorphized

One of the many ways in which metal is different from other forms of music is in its use of mascots. Oh, sure, plenty of groups in various genres have logos, from the Rolling Stones to the Wu-Tang Clan. But anthropomorphic mascots? This phenomenon is truly unique to metal.

SNAGGLETOOTH

The original metal mascot was Motörhead's Snaggletooth, a dog-boar hybrid wearing a spiked metal helmet. Snaggletooth was created by the illustrator Joe Petagno, working from Lemmy Kilmister's instructions to make "something like a knight or a rusty robot . . . a biker patch that could be displayed on the back of a denim vest." Snaggletooth graces all of the band's album covers.

EDDIE THE HEAD

Snaggletooth was the first metal mascot, but he's neither the most famous nor the best. That honor belongs to Iron Maiden's Eddie the Head. Created by legendary artist Derek Riggs, who illustrated all of Maiden's most iconic album covers, Eddie is a zombie-like creature that has become almost as important to the band as any of its members. He has appeared on all but one of the band's album covers since its eponymous 1980 debut, as well as the vast majority of its merchandise. Eddie's face has remained more or less consistent since 1981's *Killers*, when

Top to bottom: Motörhead's Snaggletooth, Megadeth's Vic Rattlehead, and Iron Maiden's Eddie the Head.

Riggs made his pupils smaller and gave him a devilish grin, making him less the undead junkie he appears to be on the cover of *Iron Maiden* and more some kind of eternal, elemental proprietor of evil. (His most prominent appearance, on the cover of 1982's *The Number of the Beast*, sees him controlling Satan like a marionette, suggesting his powers exceed even those of the Lord of the Flies.)

Unlike Snaggletooth, Eddie gets a costume change and some slight modifications from record to record, depending on the album's title and theme. Over the years he has been everything from an insane-asylum inmate to a pharaoh to a British soldier to a mummy to a cyborg. A giant Eddie even appears as part of the band's concerts, usually coming out onstage in his latest iteration to do battle with members of the band. Naturally, he has also been turned into action figures and bobbleheads and other assorted knick-knacks. Eddie also began a long tradition of metal mascots having the names of used-car salesmen, such as Murray, the massive demon utilized by Dio; Roy, Children of Bodom's version of the Grim Reaper; and Vic Rattlehead, Megadeth's mascot.

VIC RATTLEHEAD

Vic, who has become almost as well known as Eddie the Head, is a fleshless skull with steel chains affixed over its ears, steel bars jammed into its upper and lower jaw, and a steel visor screwed over its eye sockets—the ultimate metal representation of "See No Evil, Hear No Evil, Speak No Evil" (although Vic doesn't actually seem to have much difficulty seeing).

Although Megadeth mastermind Dave Mustaine created the earliest version of Vic, it was the artist Ed Repka who perfected him on the cover of 1986's classic album *Peace Sells . . . but Who's Buying?* Like Eddie, Vic's costume sometimes changes to fit a particular theme—but more often than not he's in a suit, which is befitting of Megadeth's focus on politicians and corporate leaders as the most evil people in the world. Also like Eddie, Vic sometimes makes appearances during Megadeth concerts. Still, Vic is not as omnipresent as Eddie, and at least one of Megadeth's finest releases, 1992's *Countdown to Extinction*, doesn't feature him at all.

NOT MAN

Anthrax's Not Man has the unique distinction of being the rare metal-band mascot to never adorn any the front of any the band's album covers. A misshapen, mustachioed dude with a ghoulish grin—think Luigi from Super Mario Bros., if Luigi was a circus freak and a pedophile—Not Man was modeled on a doll the band found in a Boston store. Truth be told, he is the lesser of mascots for bands featuring guitarist Scott Ian; Ian created the superior Sergeant D., a cigar-chomping skull with rotting flesh and an army helmet featuring the "anarchy" symbol, for his other project, S.O.D.

CHALY

Chaly, the horned skull with batwings that acts as the mascot for New Jersey's Overkill, was not introduced until the cover of the band's third album, *Under the Influence* (1988), but he's appeared on almost all of the band's records since. Chaly may be the only metal mascot to ever be plagiarized: Avenged Sevenfold's mascot, Deathbat, is different from Chaly only in that he has no horns. After A7X rose to prominence, Overkill released a shirt emblazoned with Chaly and the slogan, "This One's Ours . . . GET YOUR OWN FUCKING LOGO!"

There are other famous metal mascots, but they suck, and we're pressed for time.

Avenged Sevenfold's Deathbat versus Overkill's Chaly. You can tell them apart because Chaly doesn't suck. Anthrax's Not Man is opposite.

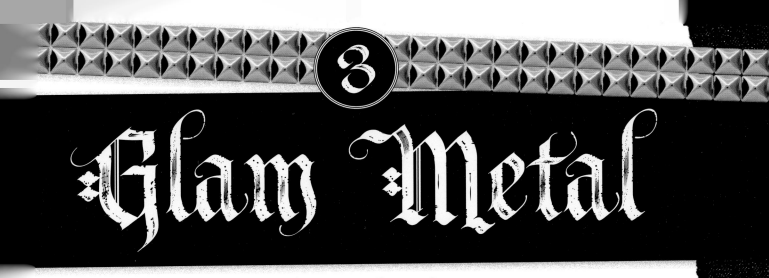

3

Glam Metal

WHAT IS IT?

Poppy, theatrical arena rock generally made by men who dress in drag.

WHO LISTENS TO IT?

People who carry pocket mirrors for the dual purpose of constantly being able to check their appearance and always having a flat surface from which they can snort cocaine.

WHERE DOES IT COME FROM?

The capital of the superficial and sleazy: Hollywood.

BASTARD CHILDREN:

None. It's hard to reproduce with hepatitis.

THE BIG FOUR:

Guns N' Roses, Mötley Crüe, Skid Row, Poison.

KISS's Paul Stanley before the age of chest waxing, circa 1975.

 f all the metallic subgenres, glam— derogatorily called "hair metal" or "cock rock"—is the one most likely to be deemed not "real" metal. The reasons for this are unsurprising: while glam utilizes some elements of more traditional forms of heavy metal (e.g., hyper-speed guitar shredding, glass-shattering falsettos, umlauts), it has always had one foot firmly planted in more mainstream forms of blues-based rock music. Metallica vocalist/guitarist James Hetfield and Mötley Crüe bassist Nikki Sixx may share a love of Aerosmith and AC/DC, but while teenage Hetfield skulked off to a friend's car to smoke weed and listen to Diamond Head, teenage Sixx snuck into a girl's window to drink and listen to Mott the Hoople.

Most forms of metal are made by social outcasts for other social outcasts; glam is made by party animals for groupies they hope to acquire.

Glam metal's unwitting progenitors were KISS and Van Halen, two bands from opposite coasts of the United States, both of whom straddled the line between heavy metal and hard rock.

KISS, from New York City, wore face paint and costumes, and each member was a distinct character: the Demon (Gene Simmons, bass/vocals), the Star Child (Paul Stanley, guitar/vocals), the Spaceman (Ace Frehley, lead guitar), and the Catman (Peter Criss, drums). Full of pyrotechnics, acrobatic wirework, and fake blood, a KISS concert is as much a Broadway show as it is a music performance.

Brothers Eddie and Alex Van Halen, from Pasadena, California, were the sons of a musician father who gave them an early start in the arts. This may account for the fact that Eddie went on to change rock guitar forever with his insane speed and revolutionary use of finger tapping. The band's other two original members were Michael Anthony, a talented high-school athlete, and David Lee Roth, an Indiana native who carried himself like the long-lost professional surfer member of the Rat Pack. It is wholly appropriate that Jeff Spiccoli, Sean Penn's legendary character from the movie *Fast Times at Ridgemont High*, is a lover of Van Halen. KISS and Van Halen both pushed the limits of what was considered "extreme" in their era, and each opened for Sabbath in the '70s. But they wrote far more melodic, radio-friendly songs than those created by their New Wave of British Heavy Metal counterparts. Their music isn't about war and death and Satan; it's about partying and getting laid. The songs for which they may be best known are called, respectively, "Rock and Roll All Nite" and "Hot for Teacher." Those titles are not metaphors.

It was a combination of elements from these two bands—theatricality; pop-tinged rock; guitar solos that seemed to cram eighteen trillion notes into a second; and lyrics celebrating sex, drugs, and rock 'n' roll—that formed the basis for glam metal.

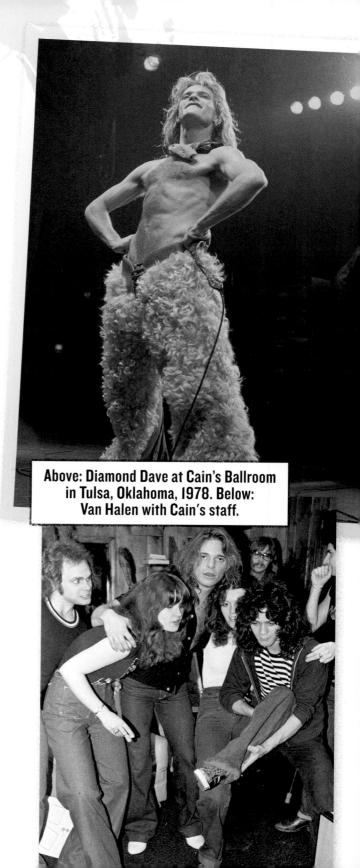

Above: Diamond Dave at Cain's Ballroom in Tulsa, Oklahoma, 1978. Below: Van Halen with Cain's staff.

Twisted Sister flunk social studies in the "I Wanna Rock" video, Los Angeles, 1984.

YOUR NAME IN LIGHTS AND YOUR ASS IN TIGHTS

The name of the game in metal is always "escalation." And so, once KISS and Van Halen had pushed rock to new heights of speed and flamboyance, the next generation was tasked with figuring out a way to kick things up a notch.

The East Coast did not fare very well in this regard. Although the region birthed plenty of fine bands in other subgenres of metal, it spawned few memorable glam metal bands. The most notable exception is New Jersey's Twisted Sister, whose legendary 1984 album, *Stay Hungry*, was a massive commercial success. It spawned two anthemic hits that are in frequent barroom and sports-event rotation to this day ("We're Not Gonna Take It" and "I Wanna Rock"), landed the band a cameo in *Pee Wee's Big Adventure*, and got the group into hot water with the Parents Music Resource Center.[1]

---

1 Led by Tipper Gore—wife of eventual vice president Al Gore—the PMRC was an organization that sought to protect the innocence of children from allegedly obscene lyrical content. The PMRC released a list, dubbed "The Filthy Fifteen," of the fifteen songs they thought best exemplified the worst in popular music. Twisted Sister was one of nine metal bands with a song included on the list, alongside AC/DC, Black Sabbath, Def Leppard, Judas Priest, Mercyful Fate, Mötley Crüe, Venom, and W.A.S.P. Twisted Sister vocalist Dee Snider famously did metal proud when he spoke passionately and articulately against the PMRC during US Senate hearings in 1985. To this day, Snider's statement is considered a landmark victory in proving that metal isn't listened to exclusively by idiots.

In true Jersey fashion, however, Twisted Sister was tongue-in-cheek and grotesque. The band's lyrics were not about smokin' babes, and while lead singer Dee Snider may have worn makeup and hot pink, pretty he was not. Twisted Sister's joyfully goofy music videos—which featured cameos from *Animal House* villain Mark "Niedermeyer" Metcalf—were often imitated by their peers; all other aspects of the band, not so much. In fact, Twisted Sister's brand of repulsive spectacle and confrontational lyrics probably had a bigger impact on underground groups than mainstream glam-rockers. The corpse paint–wearing Norwegian symphonic black-metal band Dimmu Borgir, for example, famously covered Twisted Sister's "Burn in Hell."

The other East Coast glam bands that found success, like Bon Jovi (also from New Jersey) and Cinderella (from Philadelphia), owed a far greater aesthetic debt to Hollywood than they did to Dee Snider and company. Poison, one of glam's most famous acts, was formed in Pennsylvania but didn't take off until its members relocated to Hollywood.

Parts of Europe also provided some fine glam bands, such as Hanoi Rocks (Finland) and Def Leppard (England), but, like Twisted Sister, they were mostly outliers and not part of an earnest regional scene.

Unsurprisingly, it was the young men of Los Angeles who became the true heirs to the KISS/Van Halen throne. Early examples include Quiet Riot, whose *Metal Health* (1983) went six times platinum; Ratt, whose *Out of the Cellar* (1984) went three times platinum; and Dokken, whose *Tooth and Nail* (1984), tragically, went platinum but once.

The L.A.-area outfit that perfected glam metal, however, was Mötley Crüe—a band that epitomizes all of glam's greatest strengths and garish weaknesses. The cover of its 1981 debut, *Too Fast for Love*, is a perfect visual representation of the band's entire approach to music: it's a Judas Priest-ified homage to the famous Andy Warhol cover for

Left: Quiet Riot playing Oklahoma, June 22, 1983. Below: Nikki and Vince at Madison Square Garden on the Shout at the Devil tour in 1984.

the Rolling Stones' *Sticky Fingers*, Mick Jagger's denim swapped for Crüe crooner Vince Neil's studded leather, a hypersexualized exaggeration of an already-hypersexual image.

Mötley Crüe was metal and mainstream in nearly equal measure. Over growling guitars and drumbeats that went off like bombs, Neil sang about undeniably metal topics like Satan ("Shout at the Devil"), murder ("Public Enemy #1"), hard drugs ("Dr. Feelgood"), and society's seedy underbelly ("Wild Side"). But they also recorded power ballads about broken hearts ("Without You"), party anthems about strippers ("Girls, Girls,

Girls"), and a cover of the Beatles' "Helter Skelter." One of the band's earliest hits was "Home Sweet Home," a song that opens with a quiet, lonesome piano. Three of its members had jet-black hair, but the lead singer was a blond pretty-boy who looked like David Lee Roth's Mini-Me.

GLAM METAL

Heavier, more "serious" bands like Anthrax scoffed at the very categorization of Mötley Crüe as a metal group. The Crüe, they argued, not only wrote sissy music but also emphasized style over substance.

The accusation is valid. In Mötley Crüe's collective autobiography, *The Dirt: Confessions of the World's Most Notorious Rock Band*, Nikki Sixx, the band's primary songwriter and lyricist, recalls how the group got attention early in their career:

It was just about packing people into our shows and making sure they left talking about us. . . . Vince started chain-sawing the heads off mannequins. [W.A.S.P. vocalist] Blackie Lawless had stopped lighting himself on fire [during shows] because he was tired of burning his skin, so I took over because I didn't give a shit about the pain. I would have swallowed tacks or fucked a broken bottle if it would have brought more people to our shows.

In other words, Mötley Crüe took KISS's onstage antics and multiplied them by a thousand. Drummer Tommy Lee didn't just swing through the air like Gene Simmons, he played his drum solo while suspended upside-down above the crowd. Female backup singers in skimpy outfits, respectfully ordained "Crüe Sluts," were employed for every tour. When it came to hair, there was no such thing as "too big." That none of the band members' heads ever caught on fire during a show is nothing short of a miracle.

Everything about Mötley Crüe was designed to be ultra-cool. The band's members didn't even use their real names, instead adopting sleeker-sounding stage names like "Nikki Sixx" (né Frank Serafino) and "Mick Mars" (Bob Deal). This type of vanity is in stark contrast to a band like Slayer, whose members wore jeans and T-shirts, exclusively used their real names, and aimed to awe with the extremity of their music, not their taste in attire and potentially life-threatening theatrics.

The counterargument to the assertion that Mötley Crüe's members were better showmen than they were musicians would be that their public image was mostly just a lure. This argument is also valid because, simply put, Mötley Crüe wrote amazing pop songs that just so happened to have a metallic edge. It is virtually impossible to listen to Mötley Crüe's strongest material and not walk away whistling the melody. Nikki Sixx and his bandmates may not have understood good taste, but they damn well understood good choruses.

In fact, the band's skill for churning out hits largely explains why Mötley Crüe sustained its success far longer than any of its glam-metal peers. But it's only part of the picture.

Mötley Crüe saying hi to your mom, circa 1983.

Mötley Crüe's Nikki and Vince in Oklahoma, mid '80s.

Out of all the insanely image-conscious bands to come out of Hollywood in the 1980s, the Crüe had the strongest understanding of how its audience would perceive it. The band's aesthetic, though consistently operatic, changed from album to album: they went from looking like David Bowie's *Ziggy Stardust*–era backing band to looking like they'd just stepped out of *The Road Warrior* to looking like a biker gang to wearing expensive suits. The band's logo even changed from album to album, which is rare in any genre.

Furthermore, Mötley Crüe maintained a reasonable claim to being honest-to-Lucifer badasses. Sixx famously overdosed on heroin and died for several minutes before being revived; Neil got into an accident while driving drunk that left Hanoi Rocks drummer Nicholas "Razzle" Dingley dead and two innocents grievously injured; Lee and his centerfold wife, Pamela Anderson, were one of the first celebrity couples to have a sex tape stolen and made public. And Mötley Crüe were their own best propagandists, only too happy to remind fans of their questionable behavior by any means possible, be it the aforementioned literary opus, songs like "Kickstart My Heart" (about Sixx's overdose), or titling a box set *Music to Crash Your Car To*.

The result is that Mötley Crüe's allegedly final show took place on New Year's Eve 2015 in front of 21,000 fans at the Staples Center in Los Angeles. After more than thirty years, still being able to draw that kind of crowd is an impressive feat, and one which most of the Crüe's glam peers could never even dream of.

SEX, SEX AND SEX

Mötley Crüe's success led to nearly a decade of major record labels signing basically any glam band from the Sunset Strip they could get their hands on. Some of these bands, such as Faster Pussycat, Warrant, Winger, and Slaughter, enjoyed a brief period of success, but the one that really caught on was Poison.

Which is too bad, because Poison represents glam's nadir. Its songs weren't just poppy, they were practically cotton candy. The band didn't write lyrics about Satan or drugs or being badasses. Its fashion aesthetic wasn't sexually ambiguous—it was simply effeminate. Its music videos usually consisted of the band members smiling and looking right into the camera, happily serenading

Poison with Richie Kotzen (far right), keeping it *caj*, circa 1992.

Poison at Long Beach Arena, California, April 10, 1987.

the teenage girls at home; to this day, they often perform in front of a massive backdrop featuring a picture of themselves (with lead singer Bret Michaels shirtless, natch). The band's biggest hits are about sex ("Talk Dirty to Me"), remembering sex ("I Won't Forget You"), sex ("I Want Action"), a loss of sex ("Every Rose Has Its Thorn"), and sex ("Unskinny Bop"). Its signature song is called "Nothin' but a Good Time." It's about not looking for nothin' but a good time.

Still, it's not hard to understand why Poison achieved success: its songs are catchy. Simple as that. The strongest evidence of the band's songwriting skills remains 1993's *Native Tongue*, an album made during a period when guitarist C. C. DeVille had been fired from the band (he rejoined in 1999). DeVille's replacement was the well-respected blues-rock guitarist Richie

Kotzen, whose tasteful leads and soulful vocals (he's a far better singer than Michaels) elevated the band's material to a level wherein it no longer seemed wholly ridiculous. It demonstrates that the foundations upon which Poison's music was built have always been solid—it's the decorations that are disgustingly garish.

Appetite for Delicatessen: Guns N' Roses loitering in Canter's Deli, Los Angeles, June 1985.

IF YOUR NAME WAS "SAUL," YOU'D MAKE PEOPLE CALL YOU "SLASH," TOO

Myth would have you believe that MTV stopped playing Mötley Crüe videos and started pushing Nirvana sometime within the same week. As is always the case with history, however, the fading of glam metal's dominance was a far more gradual process, with several evolutionary steps between Poison and Pearl Jam.

The first of those evolutionary steps was Guns N' Roses.

Guns N' Roses sprang forth from the same Sunset Strip scene as Poison and their ilk, and like those bands, their fashion taste leaned heavily on leather and hair spray. That was basically where the similarities to their glam peers ended. Lead guitarist Slash came from a rock 'n' roll background, his Caucasian-Jewish-British father having designed album covers for Joni Mitchell while his African-American costume-designer mother dated David Bowie; bassist Duff McKagan was primarily a punk-rocker whose hero was Sid Vicious from the Sex Pistols; rhythm guitarist Izzy

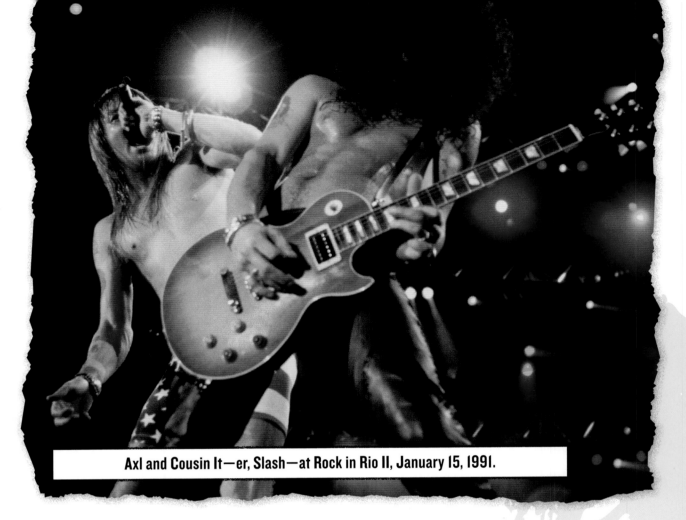

Axl and Cousin It—er, Slash—at Rock in Rio II, January 15, 1991.

Stradlin was the only one of the band's five original members to graduate from high school—with an impressive D average, no less. (The band was rounded out by Slash's grade-school chum Steven Adler on drums.)

And then there was the lead singer, Axl Rose. Rose had grown up with Stradlin in Lafayette, Indiana, in a devoutly religious home. He learned to sing in the church choir, and his stepfather, a minister, would beat him for such crimes as failing to look away when a woman on television was wearing a bathing suit. His birth father, he revealed during a 1992 *Rolling Stone* interview, was no prize either: "He kidnapped me, because someone wasn't watching me. I remember a needle. I remember getting a shot. And I remember being sexually abused by this man and watching something horrible happen to my mother when she came to get me."

When Rose turned from literal choirboy to rebel without a cause, he turned hard: he was arrested more than twenty times in Lafayette before finally following Stradlin out to Hollywood. Once there, he slept on the streets and was awoken one morning by a homeless man screaming in his face, "You know where you are?! You're in the jungle, baby! Wake up, time to die!"

Guns N' Roses lived the scumbag lifestyle most glam bands only pretended to have experienced firsthand, and Rose, in particular, was genuinely unhinged. The band members' firsthand knowledge of grime and dysfunction found its way into their music; while they may have dressed similarly to other glam bands, they sounded considerably more vicious. In a 2006 radio interview with Eddie Trunk, Rose recalled writing "Glam Sucks" on his jeans with whiteout, despite having teased hair, and taking the track "It's So Easy" in a considerably different direction from its writers' intentions:

> **"It's So Easy" was originally "the hippie ya ya song." Duff and Wes [Arkeen, a sometimes collaborator] wrote this song on acoustic [guitar] . . . and [in rehearsal] Slash basically just starts raping the song, and I ran up and started doing the evil Iggy Pop [vocals] over it . . . we just destroyed the song.**

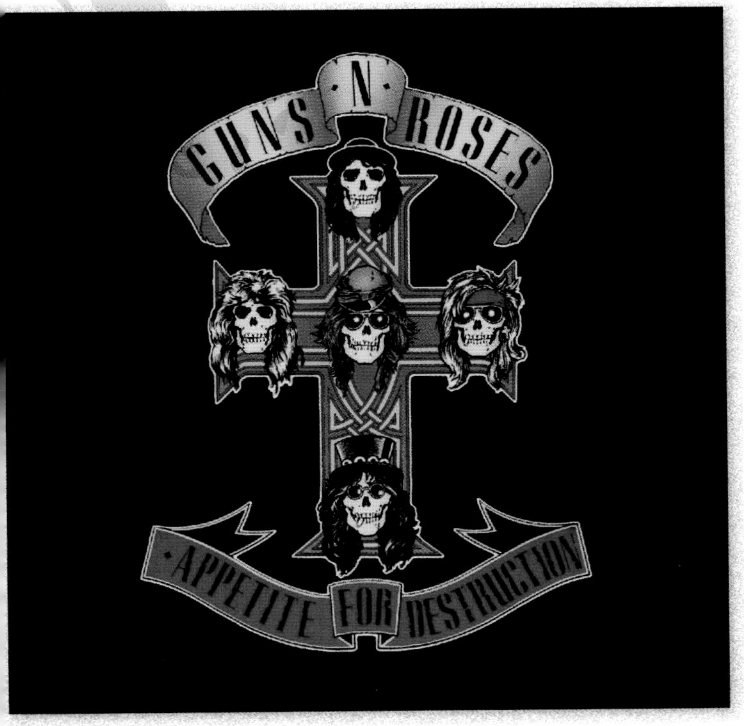

Furthermore, while Rose sometimes wrote about girls and sex, he usually wrote about being really, really emotionally fucked up. Rose's lyrics, and GN'R's entire vibe, ended up being a massive middle finger to the superficiality of the glam scene.

For proof of this, you need only compare and contrast "Cry Tough," the opening cut from Poison's debut album, *Look What the Cat Dragged In* (1986), and "Welcome to the Jungle," the opening cut from Guns N' Roses' debut album, *Appetite for Destruction* (1987). Both songs are about the challenges of seeking fame and fortune in Hollywood, but their approach is completely different.

"CRY TOUGH":

You gotta cry tough out on the streets
To make your dreams happen

"WELCOME TO THE JUNGLE":

If you got a hunger for what you see,
    you'll take it eventually
You can have anything you want, but
    you better not take it from me

Elsewhere on *Appetite for Destruction*, Rose talks about police brutality ("Out Ta Get Me"), addiction ("Mr. Brownstone"), and the falsity of American idealism ("Paradise City"). Although a sentimental semi-ballad, "Sweet Child O' Mine," was the album's breakthrough hit, it was hardly indicative of the rest of the record. When the band released a follow-up EP, *G N' R Lies*, in 1988, Rose came under fire for writing about murdering women ("Used to Love Her") and casually tossing

Bach that ass up: Skid Row, circa 1992.

out slurs against minorities and homosexuals ("One in a Million"), despite the fact that Slash was half black and Rose's self-professed favorite singers were Elton John and Queen's Freddy Mercury, both gay men.

In the years that followed, Rose became infamous for starting riots (four and counting, as of this writing!), showing up to concerts hours late, taking years to record albums, and getting into physical altercations with other celebrities. He was so short-tempered, in fact, that when he decided his bandmates had become too dependent on drugs and alcohol, he threatened to break up the band . . . publicly, in front of more than ninety thousand people, at the Los Angeles Coliseum, in the middle of a set opening for the Rolling Stones.

The combination of Rose's undeniably earnest lunacy, McKagan's punk attitude, Slash's bluesy riffs, and Stradlin's talent for turning those riffs into actual songs made Guns N' Roses unstoppable. As Chuck Klosterman writes in *Fargo Rock City: A*

Heavy Metal Odyssey in Rural North Dakota, GN'R are "the singular answer to the question, 'Why did hair metal need to exist?'" They were so goddamn good that they transcended the genre.

It's a testament to the lasting power of their work that they recorded only three LPs, one EP, and a covers album before all the band's original members save for Rose left the group in the '90s . . . and when Rose, Slash, and McKagan finally reunited in 2016, they still had no problem selling out football stadiums across the world.

Guns N' Roses ushered in an era of bands that were lumped in with glam metal, but had only minor commonalities with acts like Poison and Warrant. The most prominent example is Skid Row. The New Jersey quintet sounded decidedly meaner than other glam bands, possibly as a result of working with producer Michael Wagener, who also mixed albums by Metallica and Megadeth. The result was that Skid Row toured with glam groups like White Lion, but also with heavier acts like Pantera.

Furthermore, each Skid Row album was heavier than the one before it. By the time the band got to its third full-length album, *Subhuman Race* (1995), the glam label wasn't even appropriate anymore. That the emergence of grunge swept aside Skid Row along with the other hair-metallers was both unfortunate and unfair.

Both Florida's Saigon Kick and California's Ugly Kid Joe existed in a similar sort of limbo. Ugly Kid Joe, for example, was so named specifically to insult a glam band its members hated (Pretty Boy Floyd), and enlisted Judas Priest's Rob Halford for a guest appearance on its debut full-length, *America's Least Wanted* (1992). Somehow, though, the band got lumped in with the very glam bands its members despised. Both outfits had a couple of hits but never quite found their commercial footing in any substantial way.

The fact is, no one saw Nirvana coming—even after they arrived. The Seattle band's much-lauded breakthrough record, *Nevermind*, was released just one week after Guns N' Roses double-album opus, *Use Your Illusion I* and *II*. Skid Row wanted to take Nirvana out on tour, as did Guns N' Roses; Kurt Cobain, however, saw Rose as a misogynist brute and refused to tour with him. Naturally, this led to a very public feud with Rose, who was confused by Cobain's refusal to be lumped in with GN'R. Rose did not initially perceive a massive difference between his music and the music of Nirvana, and he saw no reason why the two bands shouldn't tour together. It's unlikely that anyone in Ratt or Cinderella ever made the same mistake.

Looking back, Rose's error seems understandable. Guns N' Roses and their ilk were the bridge from Slaughter to Smashing Pumpkins; today, they'd probably bristle at even being included in the same chapter as Faster Pussycat and Dokken.

Sorry, Axl. Please don't sue us.

Dokken playing . . . a high school, by the looks of it? Chicago, January 29, 1985.

Starter Kit

Ready to rock 'n' roll all night and party every day? You will need:

- [ ] COWBOY BOOTS, BLACK

- [ ] HEADBAND, RED

- [ ] SENSE OF MORALITY, QUESTIONABLE

- [ ] AVIATOR GLASSES WITH REFLECTIVE LENSES

- [ ] SELECT ONE (1): TORN T-SHIRT OF A BAND INFLUENTIAL ON GLAM (E.G., VAN HALEN, KISS, ETC.) OR CHEETAH-PRINT SPORTS COAT (TO BE WORN SHIRTLESS)

- [ ] SELECT ONE (1): BLACK LEATHER PANTS OR NEON SPANDEX

- [ ] RAZOR AND SHAVING CREAM (ABSOLUTELY NO HAIR BELOW THE EYELIDS PERMITTED)

- [ ] UNLIMITED SUPPLIES OF LIPSTICK, ROUGE, EYE SHADOW, EYELINER, AND COCAINE

- [ ] ONE (1) POCKET MIRROR

- [ ] ONE (1) PRESCRIPTION FOR VALTREX

Homework

1. KISS, "ROCK AND ROLL ALL NITE"
(Dressed to Kill, 1975)

2. VAN HALEN, "ERUPTION"
(Van Halen, 1978)

3. VAN HALEN, "HOT FOR TEACHER"
(1984, 1984)

4. TWISTED SISTER, "WE'RE NOT GONNA TAKE IT"
(Stay Hungry, 1984)

5. QUIET RIOT, "BANG YOUR HEAD"
(Metal Health, 1983)

6. RATT, "ROUND AND ROUND"
(Out of the Cellar, 1984)

7. DOKKEN, "INTO THE FIRE"
(Tooth and Nail, 1984)

8. W.A.S.P., "ANIMAL (FUCK LIKE A BEAST)"
(W.A.S.P., 1984)

9. MÖTLEY CRÜE, "SHOUT AT THE DEVIL"
(Shout at the Devil, 1983)

10. CINDERELLA, "SHAKE ME"
(Night Songs, 1986)

11. FASTER PUSSYCAT, "BATHROOM WALL"
(Faster Pussycat, 1987)

12. POISON, "NOTHIN' BUT A GOOD TIME"
(Open Up and Say . . . Ahh!, 1988)

13. WINGER, "SEVENTEEN"
(Winger, 1988)

14. WARRANT, "CHERRY PIE"
(Cherry Pie, 1990)

15. SLAUGHTER, "UP ALL NIGHT"
(Stick It to Ya, 1990)

16. L.A. GUNS, "SEX ACTION"
(L.A. Guns, 1988)

17. GUNS N' ROSES, "WELCOME TO THE JUNGLE"
(Appetite for Destruction, 1987)

18. SKID ROW, "MONKEY BUSINESS"
(Slave to the Grind, 1991)

19. SAIGON KICK, "HOSTILE YOUTH"
(The Lizard, 1992)

20. EXTREME, "REST IN PEACE"
(III Sides to Every Story, 1992)

21. UGLY KID JOE, "EVERYTHING ABOUT YOU"
(As Ugly As They Wanna Be, 1991)

You can almost smell the greasepaint. **KISS** at peak coolness in Chicago, Illinois, September 1979.

Yeah, who knew, right? Rob Halford, in 1979, before he came out.

Sexuality in Metal: Pride the Lightning

The metalhead stereotype is that of a homophobic straight male with unrealistic ideas about women. This is not an entirely incorrect cliché, though it is becoming more and more outdated every year. During its rise to mainstream attention, heavy metal was classless in its portrayal of sex, which was filled with fantasy scenarios where muscle-bound hulks rescued top-heavy damsels. Metal lyrics were either about missing kind, proper lovers, or taming bad ones (who were all the sexier for their dysfunction).

If statistics are to be believed, one in ten people is attracted to members of the same sex, and if that's true then there must be quite a few gay and bisexual metalheads. Yet to this day, many heavy metal fans and musicians are outwardly hostile toward homosexuality and gay culture. For some, this comes from the feeling that their toughness is in question (toughness rather than masculinity, because while the majority of homophobic metalheads are men, anyone who's attended a metal show will tell you that there are plenty of women ready to spew the word "faggot" at you). For others, it's a sense of adherence to musical tradition—dudes like Manowar stayed true to metal and wrote about bedding hot chicks. Therefore, to be straight is to be metal.

And yet Manowar's album covers

consistently feature the male body as centerpiece. Any women present, such as the demonic porno models on the cover of 1992's *The Triumph of Steel,* are usually fighting for attention from a piece of beefcake who seems preoccupied with flexing. Manowar's most famous track is named "Brothers of Metal Pt. I," its title suggesting that metal is only enjoyed in the company of other men. ("Siblings of Metal" isn't quite as catchy, but still, there has been no follow-up about metal sisters.) Manowar's muscle-magazine imagery seems to suggest that it takes a real man to be obsessed with other real men.

Everything changed when Judas Priest vocalist Rob "Metal God" Halford came out in 1998. Halford's lyrics portrayed sex as a power dynamic, a grossly violent act between "bodies revvin' in leather" full of "gut-wrenching frenzy that deranges every joint." To discover that he was writing these lyrics about other men meant that any metal lyric about sex, no matter how grandiose or filthy, was up for

arguments about how only real men could play metal were proven entirely false—if Halford was gay, then being gay was in no way a detriment to being metal. Thankfully, the metal community managed to be decent that time around and rallied behind Halford for his honesty and bravery in the face of an often cruel and stupid world.

Because it's perceived as erotic by straight men, lesbianism is more accepted in metal culture—but that, of course, creates a whole new set of problems.

"I don't think anyone told Rob Halford that he just hadn't had the right pussy yet," says Otep Shamaya. The frontwoman for aggro metallers Otep, Shamaya has had to deal with her fair share of idiotic shit in the name of her sexuality. "When we were first on Ozzfest, plenty of bands were intimidated by me being a woman and getting better responses from crowds. The one thing they could jab at me about was not what we did onstage, but that I was gay. Early on, I thought that [extreme music] is a place for exiles. But suddenly you're only an exile if you act like everybody else. That was really disappointing to me—wait a minute, we're supposed to be the gap culture that society kicked out on the streets, the freaks! That was not really the case." In Shamaya's eyes, the insults hurled at her for her sexuality were at their core about gender insecurities. "There's a certain idea of what a woman should be, in music and in life. And it's not just men who think that, women do, too. You don't need men to build a patriarchy—plenty of women will do it themselves. I can't tell you how many times I've been told to tone it down onstage. Not my rhetoric, my energy."

As views on sexuality change in society at large, they change in metal. More and more metal musicians have come out of the closet, including Gorgoroth's ultra-satanic frontman Gaahl and Cynic's prog-minded drummer and guitarist, Sean Reinert and Paul Masvidal. In the early 2000s, Marissa Martinez, front woman for the band Cretin, came out as the first prominent transgender metal musician, followed soon after by Mina Caputo of Life of Agony. Otep has seen the shift first-hand among her fans. "We wrote a song called 'Equal Right Equal Left.' It's about LGBTQ rights, and it's been the most popular song that we've ever released. The minute we played it onstage, the fans went crazy for it. We play it no matter where we play. The response is always positive."

At the same time, plenty of musicians make a point of callously expressing conservative views on sexuality and gender. Megadeth's Dave Mustaine has made it clear that his religion keeps him from approving of gay marriage, and All That Remains frontman Phil Labonte is known for casually hurling homophobic slurs on social media; Labonte claims he's showing the importance of words, seemingly to make up for his inability to express it elsewhere.

Idiotically, sexuality in metal remains a controversial issue, but more and more those people hoisting the flag of prejudice and ignorance are being seen for what they are—super-dumb and kind of whiny. For her own LGBTQ fans, Otep offers the following advice: "Be loud, be proud. Be strong. Know that there are people out there just like you, fighting for you. There are places to go, bands to reach out to. They are unafraid, they will never back down."

Gaahl of Gorgoroth and God Seed, extreme metal's gay icon.

Henry Rollins and Black Flag, May 22, 1985. Holy shit.

A Crash Course in Hardcore

Hardcore punk, usually just called "hardcore," is a form of heavy music that is a lot like punk, only more hardcore. Thus the name.

The genre's roots go back to the late '70s/early '80s. Conservatism was on the rise, thanks to the election of world leaders like President Ronald Reagan and Prime Minister Margaret Thatcher. Concurrently, punk had lost its edge and become mainstream, co-opted by art's ever-present nemesis, the Suits. In response to this began a movement of young bands looking to step up punk's game and restore its street cred. Groups including Hermosa Beach's Black Flag, D.C.'s Bad Brains, L.A.'s Circle Jerks, NYC's Agnostic Front, and England's Discharge strove to bring back the authenticity and anti-corporate, DIY work ethic punk lost.

Thus, like the Norwegian black-metal movement a decade later, the hardcore scene took shit rrrrrreeeeaaaalllllyyy seriously. For example, although there was a noticeable overlap in the metal and hardcore fan base, hardcore dudes shaved their heads, and having long hair at a hardcore show was grounds for an ass-whooping. In fact, hardcore shows were generally not a great place for anyone viewed as a "poseur."

Hardcore is as ferocious musically as it is philosophically, taking punk to new levels of furious discord. Punk says you don't have to be a good singer because there's purity in sloppy

H.R. of Bad Brains, circa 1986.

vocals; hardcore says you don't have to be a good singer because everything is gonna be screamed. The influence of classic rock 'n' roll is still readily apparent in punk; hardcore is all about speed and aggression, and may or may not have a hook.

Other notable contributions hardcore made to heavy music include the D-beat, a relatively simple alternation between the kick and snare drums played at a breakneck speed; gang shouts (phrases shouted by multiple people);

and moshing, a form of not-dancing in which people run and push and crash into each other. The sections of venue floors dedicated to these activities are known as "mosh pits," or simply "pits" (as in, "The pit last night was in-SANE, bruh!"). In the decades since the advent of the mosh, the form has birthed multiple variations, including the circle pit, in which fans run in one massive circle, as if to conjure a tornado of sweat and body odor, and so-called "karate moshing," in which people nobody likes flail their limbs around like a child imitating Bruce Lee, regardless of their proximity to other human beings.

Hardcore has also spawned several stringent sub-movements, including a scene devoted to being "straight edge," meaning drug- and alcohol-free (Minor Threat, 7 Seconds, Youth of Today, Judge, etc.). Syracuse's environmentally conscientious straight-edge band Earth Crisis took things so far that its fans were known to lay out fellow concertgoers for smoking cigarettes.

Meanwhile, Houston's D.R.I. (Dirty Rotten Imbeciles), Raleigh's C.O.C. (Corrosion of Conformity), New York's S.O.D. (Stormtroopers of Destruction), and other initials-loving bands created the subgenre known as "crossover thrash," or simply "crossover," so named because it melds hardcore and thrash music (see Thrash Metal, page 93).

Crossover thrash created a safe space for metal dudes to go see hardcore bands without fear of ending their night in the back of an ambulance. Consequently, Guns N' Roses and Slayer each made albums of hardcore covers (1993's *The Spaghetti Incident?* and 1996's *Undisputed Attitude*, respectively), while bands such as Refused, from Sweden, began to mix the two styles even more freely. This,

in turn, helped to blur the lines between metal and hardcore, which led to the creation of hybrid genres such as "grindcore" (page 123) and "metalcore" (page 233), which resulted in simply tagging the "core" suffix to basically any other word when attempting to christen a particular scene (e.g., deathcore, fashioncore, Sumeriancore, Christcore, gamecore, gorecore).

Although there is definitely still a pure hardcore movement today, the distinction between the various styles of extreme music dubbed "core" has never been murkier. Certain bands that utilize elements of both styles, such as Converge and the Dillinger Escape Plan, would probably object to us including them in the chapter on the New Wave of American Heavy Metal/Metalcore rather than here. It's a nebulous line, and truth be told, there are scores of modern bands that do not fit simply into one genre or the other.

Extra Credit

1. BLACK FLAG, "RISE ABOVE"
(Damaged, 1981)

2. BAD BRAINS, "BANNED IN D.C."
(Bad Brains, 1982)

3. MISFITS, "LAST CARESS"
(Beware, 1980)

4. D.R.I., "TEAR IT DOWN"
(Crossover, 1987)

5. REFUSED, "NEW NOISE"
(The Shape of Punk to Come, 1998)

Thrash Metal

WHAT IS IT?

Fast and *tight* punk-fueled dancing
metal with misanthropic themes.

WHO LISTENS TO IT?

Excitable indoor kids who deal with their ADHD-driven
awkwardness by getting fucked up and skateboarding.

WHERE DOES IT COME FROM?

The San Francisco Bay Area, the outer boroughs
of New York, Germany, and South America.

BASTARD CHILDREN:

Black thrash, neo-thrash, revival thrash,
toxic thrash, power thrash, deathrash, technical thrash,
aggro-thrash, crossover thrash, witching metal.

THE BIG FOUR:

Metallica, Slayer, Anthrax, Megadeth.
(Fun fact: This is the original Big Four, the one this stat
is named after. Way to read a book, pal.)

Metallica running late for remedial Spanish, in 1985.

bove all things, thrash saved metal from being lame. It made metal angry, and by doing so rescued the genre from complete and total geekdom forever.

Sure, the technical talent and hedonism of the New Wave of British Heavy Metal was fun and compelling, but it was also mid-paced, self-indulgent, and a bit too obsessed with Tolkienish tales of orcs and elves. Punk and hardcore, meanwhile, thrived on a very real sense of nihilism and bristling aggression, and got people moving. Behind all of this was the Cold War paranoia of the 1980s, the many ongoing advancements of the day backlit with an understanding that sociopathic socialites might execute every living creature on earth with the push of a button.

Metal had the riff and the myth. Punk brought the anger and speed. Society provided the nuclear holocaust. A terrifying beast was born.

"First and foremost, thrash is about the energy," says Rob Cavestany, lead guitarist for Bay Area thrashers Death Angel. For many, Death Angel are the embodiment of the thrash scene's longevity—the members were all of fifteen when the band formed in 1982, and they've continued making solid moshing music ever since. "It's pissed off, but from where we're coming from, we let out angst and anger and frustration, but in a positive way. It's a total release. You get shit out of your system in a way that's not just punching a hole in the wall. It's a unity of people letting it all out, but in a friendly way."

It helped that thrash kids had something to rebel against. On the Sunset Strip, former jocks wearing mascara were topping the charts with sugarcoated anthems about getting laid, which to most metalheads seemed like more of a fantasy than the apocalypse. In response, thrash kids rocked utilitarian biker clothing like tight jeans, patched-up vests, sneakers, and T-shirts. Old-school Motörhead-worship and a penchant for barbarians allowed for spiked leather and bullet belts.

As thrash became self-aware, it went from underground noise for ugly people to the metal that mattered most. The forward-thinking politics and cultural paranoia behind the music made it more relevant and palatable than the gross sexual innuendos and endless rhyming of "self" with "shelf" that dominated mainstream '80s metal. And while glam got steadily softer in an attempt to remain commercially viable, thrash provided listeners with the solid riffs for which they came to metal in the first place.

It also helps when a genre spawns the greatest metal band of all time.

One doubts that Lars Ulrich and James Hetfield knew what was happening when the latter responded to the former's ad in the *Recycler*. Ulrich was a potential tennis pro who'd lived in Denmark until he was sixteen and was clued into European underground progenitors like Mercyful Fate and Venom. Hetfield was the son of Christian Scientists whose family's refusal to use medicine resulted in the death of his mother, Cynthia, when he was a teenager. Ulrich's friendship with Metal Blade Records founder Brian Slagel resulted in his then-unknown band getting its song "Hit the Lights" onto the label's *Metal Massacre* compilation. In October of '81, the boys were joined by guitar wizard and bitterness pioneer Dave Mustaine (we'll get to him), and Metallica was formed.

Though *Metal Massacre* announced the group to the world, Metallica was not yet complete. First, the others had to be joined by Cliff Burton, the

James Hetfield and Kirk Hammett going full *Kaiju* at Shibuya Public Hall, Tokyo, November 1986.

hippie-punk bassist who would convince the guys to move to the San Francisco Bay Area. Second, they needed to replace Mustaine, whose drinking and drug use was out of control (and given that the band was nicknamed "Alcoholica," Dave must've been *sooome* dick while he was wasted). The band was recording in New York when Dave got the boot, and since his bandmates had no money, Mustaine was forced to take a bus all the way back to California. That afternoon, they hired guitarist Kirk Hammett away from Exodus.

This is the Metallica lineup that would take over the world and record the band's three greatest albums: 1983's *Kill 'Em All*, 1984's *Ride the Lightning*, and 1986's *Master of Puppets*. Though the first two didn't take off immediately, they built the band a loyal underground following. *Master of Puppets*, meanwhile, was a thrilling success, filled with the infectious riffs and gritty realism so many other metal bands lacked. The album took Metallica from a band of niche weirdoes to gods of the genre.

What set Metallica apart from its peers was, for lack of a better word, honesty. Like Motörhead's before it, Metallica's music sounded as though it was wrenched out of a human heart rather than a Dungeons & Dragons *Monster Manual*. Hetfield and Hammett weaved agonizing guitar solos between unforgettable riffs, while Hetfield's vocals sounded like nothing more than a metalhead screaming. The few times the band branched into fantasy, it was for instrumental retellings of H. P. Lovecraft stories or the Passover story told from the point of view of the Angel of Death ("The Call of Ktulu" and "Creeping Death," respectively).

Things were looking up for Metallica. Then, on September 27, 1986, the band's tour bus hit a patch of black ice on a highway outside Dorarp, Sweden.

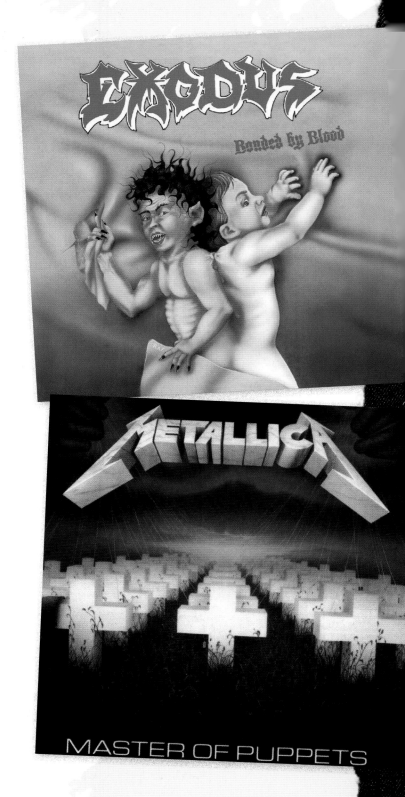

Metallica, circa 1991: new bassist Jason Newsted, far right, assuming things will get better.

The bus crashed. Cliff died.

Losing Burton changed Metallica irreparably; it quickly became clear that Cliff was the band's heart, and his passing crushed his brothers in arms. He was swiftly replaced with Flotsam and Jetsam bass player Jason Newsted, whom Ulrich, Hammett, and Hetfield reportedly tormented in a never-ending hazing ritual that was really an outlet for their grief over losing a friend.

The band made its most ambitious album to date, . . . *And Justice For All*, in 1988. As part of his "new guy" gauntlet, Newsted's bass was entirely mixed out. From this record came the song "One," based on Dalton Trumbo's novel *Johnny Got His Gun*, about a soldier who loses his arms, legs, vision, hearing, and ability to speak in a landmine explosion. The video for "One," which includes footage from the film adaptation of *Johnny Got His Gun*, did heavy rotation on MTV, officially making the band public darlings.

Metallica followed up *Justice* with its 1991 self-titled record, colloquially known as *The Black Album* due to its jet-black cover, which saw the group trading thrash for straightforward biker rock. The album was produced by Bob Rock, who was fresh off of his work with Mötley Crüe and the Cult; though some fans saw the alliance as sleeping with the enemy, many considered it an announcement to the world that Metallica would never again play anywhere smaller than a stadium or festival.

Lars, Cliff, and James of Metallica, all looking about seven years old at the Aardshock Festival in the Netherlands, 1984.

The album's opener, "Enter Sandman," was a gigantic single, its video also becoming an MTV staple. But the resulting financial windfall and emotional constipation over Burton made the dudes in Metallica the things they once hated. They cut their hair and appeared in crushed velvet and animal print. They spoke out loudly against the music-sharing platform Napster, disavowing their younger bootleg-encouraging selves. Worst of all, they wrote grunge-inflected hard-rock tunes with no solos in an attempt to stay relevant in the changing music scene. All of this culminated in 2003's *St. Anger*, a botched return to form featuring what sounds like Lars Ulrich playing a frying pan with another frying pan. Most fans consider *Anger* the worst metal album of all time, and it's hard to argue with them.

Thankfully, this is not where Metallica's story ends. Soon after *St. Anger*'s release, the band replaced Newsted with Robert Trujillo, bassist for Ozzy Osbourne's solo band and crossover thrashers Suicidal Tendencies, whose energetic nature and continued dedication to underground metal seemed to reinvigorate the others. They dropped *Some Kind of Monster*, a documentary about *St. Anger*'s creation that shows Metallica dealing with alcoholism, loss, and Ulrich's disapproving, Odin-look-alike father. With new blood and their demons (somewhat) exorcised, Metallica bounced back, releasing two consecutive returns to form: 2008's *Death Magnetic* and 2016's *Hardwired . . . To Self-Destruct!* Metal's greatest band will never regain its former glory, but at least its members have climbed shakily back to their feet.

Megadeth, circa 1986.

I'LL SHOW THEM!
I'LL SHOW THEM ALL!

As Metallica went from speedy opening act to arena headliner, thrash metal changed around them. Other major players were emerging, pushing the boundaries of speed and extremity in an attempt to compete with the shifting landscape of the sonic underworld.

"We were really young at the time, and getting mentored by guys like Metallica and Exodus," says Cavestany. "It was our version of going to play football—you're trying to throw people down, but in a fun way. It's primeval but artistic at the same time. I mean, just like everyone else, there were some people in there who were negative about it. There's always some asshole at the football game ruining it for everyone else."

Dave Ellefson of Megadeth acting out how it feels to work with Dave Mustaine, circa 1986.

Dave Mustaine had a long bus ride from New York back to California to think about getting even with his old bandmates in Metallica. Two months after his dismissal, the guitarist reemerged with Megadeth, a band in which he wanted to play faster, louder, and heavier music than Metallica's. While many have argued about whether or not he achieved his goal, Mustaine's mastery of the guitar is an unquestionable fact, and Megadeth certainly surpassed his former band in terms of technical acrobatics, showcasing uncommon rhythms and hard-to-wrangle riffs.

Megadeth embodied a core thrash mindset of political disenfranchisement and cynicism. The band straddled reality and fantasy, writing songs about possible-but-not-likely topics like Area 51 and being trapped in an insane asylum. Mustaine's very guitar tone on classics like 1986's *Peace Sells . . . But Who's Buying?* and 1990's *Rust in Peace* has a mechanical quality that makes one think of artificial intelligence and video game mutants rather than, say, Lucifer's legions of death. The band's mascot, Vic Rattlehead, is a suit-clad skeleton that can hear, see, and speak no evil thanks to surgically applied steel plates.

But though it has a loyal fan base that sees it as thrash's greatest achievement, Megadeth has always been a fraught project (unsurprising, given that the band was formed almost entirely as a revenge tactic). Mustaine's continued drinking and drug use made him a volatile frontman who soon became as difficult to work with as he was musically gifted. The band's lineup was in a constant state of flux since its inception, with Mustaine the only stable member.

Megadeth continued onward, succumbing to the great dull-down of the 1990s. Mustaine

eventually sobered up but revealed a controversial love of Christianity and conservative politics, taking time to question President Obama's birthplace in 2012 and announcing that African women with too many children should "plug it up." As a result, critically acclaimed Megadeth albums like 2016's *Dystopia* are often received by liberal fans with a raised eyebrow, while drek like 2013's *Super Collider* gives naysayers ample ammunition with which to shit on Mustaine and his band.

Anthrax, the thrash metal Beach Boys, Milwaukee, Wisconsin, April 26, 1989.

STOMP THE PAIN AWAY

Given thrash's love of street music like hardcore and hip-hop, it was inevitable that New York would get in on the game, which it did in the form of Anthrax from Queens. Formed by guitarist Scott Ian and bassist Dan Lilker, Anthrax was completed by charismatic drummer Charlie Benante, bassist Frank Bello (Benante's nephew, strangely enough, who joined when Lilker quit the band), guitarist Dan Spitz, and vocalist Neil Turbin. The band's 1984 album, *Fistful of Metal,* is a genre classic, partly for its iconic cover art, which features a chain-wrapped fist smashing its way out of someone's mouth. But it was only after Turbin was replaced by the perpetually tan Joey Belladonna that Anthrax shone, releasing monumental records like 1985's *Spreading the Disease* and 1987's *Among the Living*.

"A great song is a great song, no matter where it was written," says Frank Bello. While some might hear Anthrax's music and think rabid catharsis, Bello is a font of positivity when discussing the genre. "The Big Four was a celebration of us coming up together. It was more about tunnel vision, and doing what's in your stomach. We're diehard music fans—we love Maiden and Priest; we grew up with that stuff. Our music is a tribute to that. We never stopped being fans of this music. I feel very fortunate to be in metal while it's stronger than ever."

In the friend group of the Big Four, Anthrax is the chill dude who everyone feels like they can talk to. Belladonna's wailing vocals were reminiscent of the metal that thrash musicians grew up with, while Ian's wide-eyed stomping and shaved head connected with the hardcore kids and skate punks.

MTV loved the shorts-clad skater-metal dudes in the band and even sponsored a contest in which the group destroyed the winners' home (the concept later became part of an episode of *Married . . . with Children* in which the band made a cameo).

Anthrax broke metal's perceived race barrier by touring with hardcore rap crew Public Enemy and collaborating with them on the rap-metal progenitor "Bring the Noise." All that, and it still made some of the best thrash of the '90s, with Armored Saint's John Bush replacing Belladonna and bringing a more grating vocal style to the band's sound on records like 1993's *Sound of White Noise* and 2003's *We've Come for You All*. These days, Belladonna is back in the band and singing on some of Anthrax's most successful music to date, with 2016's *For All Kings* taking high slots on many critics' "Album of the Year" lists.

"It takes a never-say-die attitude," says Bello. "Maybe it's a New York mentality. You can never take no for an answer. When we wanted to change things, people said no. Even today, with these two recent records, people said, 'You can never come back,' and we did. Don't listen to other people, just make your own way."

Anthrax pioneered a vital subset of the thrash movement, crossover thrash. Young headbangers might be surprised to learn that in the '80s, metal and hardcore were at odds. Punks saw metalheads as indulgent longhairs who sang about nerdy bullshit, and metalheads saw punks as dickhead loudmouths who couldn't play their instruments. But Anthrax's mix of mosh-along riffs, metal yells, and good times made its shows the perfect place for metal and hardcore kids to bro down. The movement soon spawned dozens of bands, including Nuclear Assault (featuring former Anthrax bassist Dan Lilker), Suicidal Tendencies, Cryptic Slaughter, Cro-Mags, Biohazard, and Carnivore from Brooklyn, whose towering frontman Pete Steele would make his biggest influence on metal crooning about dead women (see A Crash Course in Goth Metal, page 145).

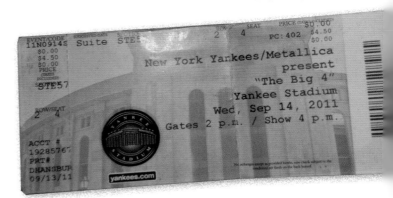

They're smiling. That's . . . not good. Fucking Slayer, circa 1986.

HELL YES

So you had Metallica, who were for everyone; Megadeth, who were for the societal know-it-alls; and Anthrax, who were for fun-loving skaters.

Then you had Slayer.

Even though their music sounds like someone holding a chainsaw having a seizure, Slayer is perhaps the most famous underground band in the world. Its mixture of Judas Priest's steel-plated war stories and Venom's tact-to-the-wind Satanism won over all the scary fuck-ups of the world. While Metallica inspired the future generation of hard-rock stars, Slayer single-handedly created death and black metal with its paeans to serial murder, blood-drenched battlefields, and the Devil.

In fact, Slayer's very name is a widely accepted battle cry in the metal community. Why don't we try it right now? Wherever you are, throw back your head and repeat after me:

SSSLAAAAAYEEEEEEEEERRR!

Feels good, right? Congratulations, your guardian angel just threw up.

Slayer's terrifying reputation is based almost entirely around the ferocity of its music; unlike Mötley Crüe, Slayer does not have a book's worth of drug use and burrito musk to be scary on its behalf. The band's history is kind of uneventful—high-school valedictorian Kerry King and World War II–obsessed punker Jeff Hanneman met when they were teenagers and joined up with Chilean-American singer Tom Araya and Cuban-American drum monster Dave Lombardo. The band wrote multiple evil-ass albums until it was picked up by famed hip-hop producer Rick Rubin, who helped them make the thirty-minute thrash masterpiece *Reign in Blood*. The band's greatest tragedy was Hanneman's death from alcohol-related liver failure in 2013.

So how did Slayer become Slayer in the eyes of the world? Maybe it was leaving Metal Blade to sign with Rubin's rap label, Def Jam, showing the metal scene that the group was more militant than its poofy-haired counterparts. Maybe it was the band members' dabbling in Nazi subject matter and aesthetics—the *S* in the Slayer logo undoubtedly resembles that used by Hitler's Secret Service, and *Reign in Blood*'s opening track, "Angel of Death," describes in great detail the horrors perpetrated by Nazi scientist Josef Mengele.

Slayer with legendary producer Rick Rubin, celebrating the release of 2001's *God Hates Us All*, September 10, 2001.

At the end of the day, however, what Slayer did better than anyone else was evil. Metal had already sold its soul by the time Slayer came around—Black Sabbath had been seduced by evil on "N.I.B.," King Diamond recited Anton LaVey's *Satanic Bible* in piercing falsetto, and Venom enjoyed banging zombie chicks in hell. But Slayer saw hell as a state of mind related to the cultural psyche. Songs like "Chemical Warfare," "Hell Awaits," "Born of Fire," and the punishing earworm of "Raining Blood" took diabolism in bizarre subliminal directions, more like the disjointed paintings of Hieronymus Bosch than any Bible story. In short, they were deadly serious about what they did, and for a specific type of kid, who saw Beelzebub in the smile of every baby and blood bubbling up in every gutter, it was the music that finally made them feel whole.

Of course, being only human, the members of Slayer eventually failed to live up to their reputations as murderous acolytes of Lucifer. They publicly admitted that their fascination with the occult was fascination alone, leaving them with only sex, murder, and battlefield mutilation to write about.

Machine Head, in 1995. Not pictured: a facial hair stylist putting his kids through college.

...AND OTHER BACK PATCHES YOU MIGHT HAVE SEEN

While Metallica and Slayer were the forward faces of the Bay Area scene, a slew of rabid bands were creating sonic beat-downs of their own. Exodus, from which Metallica once upon a time stole guitarist Kirk Hammett, became every thrasher's favorite second-tier band, the off-kilter enthusiasm of sadly deceased frontman Paul Baloff adding a devil-may-care attitude to its music. Testament, meanwhile, focused on catchier songwriting and displayed thrash's maturing chops on albums like 1988's *The New Order* and 1989's *Practice What You Preach*. Dark Angel rejected the NWOBHM worship of those that came before in favor of no-frills speed and fury. Meanwhile, on the East Coast, Anthrax's more traditional heavy metal vibe was carried on by New Jersey's Overkill.

But the United States wasn't having all the fun. In Canada, Anvil firmly straddled the line between classic power metal and speedy thrash, while Voivod transformed its brand of sloppy speed metal into wonky prog-metal. Germany spawned three of thrash's most important bands, Kreator, Destruction, and Sodom, who, fueled by icy European power metal and hard-edged German hardcore, wrote humorless riffs and war-mongering lyrics that would heavily inspire black and death metal bands.

In Switzerland, a young Tom Gabriel Fisher was releasing a series of creepy and unhinged EPs under the name Hellhammer; that band transformed into Celtic Frost, an obsidian juggernaut that took thrash to atmospheric and avant-garde extremes inspired by the art of fellow countrymen and *Alien* designer H. R. Giger. Fisher,

Sepultura at Donington Park, Derby, England, 1994.

casually known as Tom G. Warrior, was a disciple of Venom, and he crafted a guitar tone that sounded like an ax blade made out of volcanic rock.

Hellhammer's pitch-black sloppiness and Celtic Frost's grand scope combined to form what we think of as black metal; at the time of their formation, no one had any idea what to do with them. Even further abroad, in Brazil, brothers Max and Iggor Cavalera decided to make their own music in reverence of Destruction and Hellhammer. Their band, Sepultura, boiled thrash down to its key components; they released two stark albums that would define death metal (1989's *Beneath the Remains* and 1991's *Arise*) and two that

informed the primal kinetic energy of nu metal (1993's *Chaos A.D.* and 1996's *Roots*).

While everyone likes to believe that all metal died during the '90s, thrash merely mutated. Since thrash was considered culturally valuable and somewhat intelligent, it couldn't be totally dismissed. Bands like Pantera adopted more groove and Southern swing into their bikerish riffs (see A Crash Course in Groove Metal and Sludge, page 172), while Vio-lence guitarist Robb Flynn started the immensely popular act Machine Head. Strapping Young Lad, fronted by Steve Vai guitarist/vocalist and sonic gadabout Devin Townsend, merged shimmering industrial with clinical thrash riffs to create a tight but volatile sound. SYL's 1997 album *City* is about as perfect as they come, a seething cortex of electricity and anxiety.

That said, by the year 2000, death metal had emerged as the fastest, most unlistenable metal around, and black metal's No Fun Satanism and legit criminal record made the dudes in Slayer look tamer than ever. But what this did was make thrash difficult to find and rewarding for those who sought it out. And no one loves buried treasure quite like a metalhead.

The 2000s saw a new legion of thrash bands emerge—young bucks who just wanted to make the music their older brothers had introduced them to. Underground European acts like Carnal Forge and Witchery got the ball rolling, while bands like Richmond's Municipal Waste, Portland's Toxic Holocaust, and Northern Ireland's Gama Bomb used killer riffs to reinvigorate old-school topics like beer, pizza, and radioactive zombies. Many metalheads became quickly exhausted by the thrash revival and the glut of questionable bands it spawned, but eventually warmed to darker, harder acts like Power Trip from Austin, Texas, and masked Creepsylvanian crushers Ghoul, whose music was less about '80s pop-culture references and more about finding your teeth after the show.

These days, thrash is a nostalgic chapter in metal's history, a sweaty party that every headbanger wishes they could've attended. But these reminiscences often forget the point of thrash: it saved metal from itself. One more stupid, clichéd description of a castle or wizard, and metal would've been dead in the water. Thrash, with its fire and speed and pessimism, pulled metal out of its own ass and tossed it into the pit.

Starter Kit

Ready to get caught in a mosh?
You will need:

- ☐ 32 OZ. JACK AND COKE IN A SUPER BIG GULP CUP
- ☐ $1.28 WORTH OF GOOEY FAST FOOD
- ☐ ONE (1) T-SHIRT, SLEEVELESS
- ☐ ONE (1) PAIR JEANS, 32 IN. WAIST
- ☐ ONE (1) DENIM JACKET, SLEEVELESS
- ☐ SIX (6) BAND PATCHES TO BE SEWN ONTO JEANS
- ☐ TWO (2) PAIRS SNEAKERS, WHITE
- ☐ THREE (3) TATTOOS: NUCLEAR, SATANIC, AND A
  1980S CARTOON CHARACTER
- ☐ HIGH BLOOD SUGAR

Homework

1. TESTAMENT, "INTO THE PIT"
(The New Order, 1988)

2. DEATH ANGEL, "THRASHERS"
(The Ultra-Violence, 1987)

3. EXODUS, "STRIKE OF THE BEAST"
(Bonded by Blood, 1985)

4. SLAYER, "NECROPHILIAC"
(Hell Awaits, 1983)

5. ANTHRAX, "I AM THE LAW"
(Among the Living, 1987)

6. METALLICA, "MASTER OF PUPPETS"
(Master of Puppets, 1986)

7. OVERKILL, "BLOOD MONEY"
(Horrorscope, 1991)

8. KREATOR, "FLAG OF HATE"
(Endless Pain, 1985)

9. DESTRUCTION, "INVINCIBLE FORCE"
(Infernal Overkill, 1985)

10. NUCLEAR HOLOCAUST, "INHERITED HELL"
(Handle with Care, 1989)

11. MEGADETH, "HOLY WARS . . . THE PUNISHMENT DUE"
(Rust in Peace, 1990)

12. DARK ANGEL, "MERCILESS DEATH"
(Darkness Descends, 1986)

13. SODOM, "AUSGEBOMBT"
(Agent Orange, 1989)

14. SLAYER, "MANDATORY SUICIDE"
(South of Heaven, 1988)

15. CELTIC FROST, "NECROMANTICAL SCREAMS"
(To Mega Therion, 1985)

16. CARNIVORE, "GROUND ZERO BROOKLYN"
(Retaliation, 1987)

17. VOIVOD, "THE UNKNOWN KNOWS"
(Nothing Face, 1989)

18. SEPULTURA, "ARISE"
(Arise, 1991)

19. STRAPPING YOUNG LAD, "DETOX"
(City, 1997)

20. MACHINE HEAD, "DAVIDIAN"
(Burn My Eyes, 1994)

21. WITCHERY, "WICKED"
(Symphony for the Devil, 2001)

22. MUNICIPAL WASTE, "HEADBANGER FACE RIP"
(The Art of Partying, 2007)

23. TOXIC HOLOCAUST, "NOWHERE TO RUN"
(Conjure and Command, 2011)

24. GHOUL, "DEATH CAMPAIGN"
(Dungeon Bastards, 2016)

25. POWER TRIP, "EXECUTIONER'S TAX (SWING OF THE AXE)"
(Nightmare Logic, 2017)

26. METALLICA, "ENTER SANDMAN"
(Metallica, 1991)

The late Chris Cornell bringing it to the crowd at a *RIP Magazine* party, October 5, 1991.

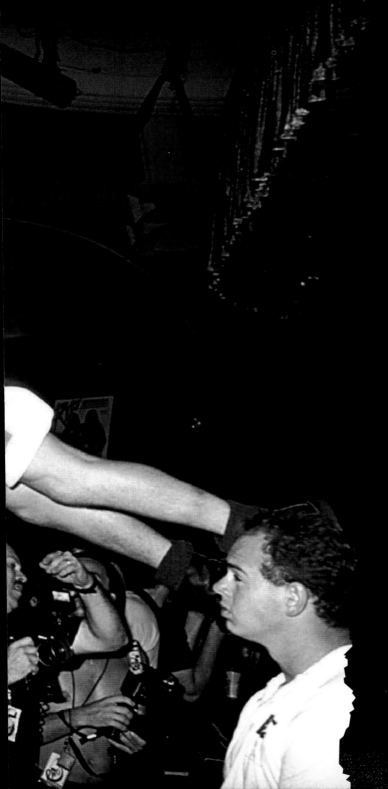

A Crash Course in Alternative Metal

"Alternative" is a catchall meant to describe any artist too weird for the mainstream. It became a common-use term in the early '90s, when a subset of alternative called "grunge" became popular, thanks to the success of Nirvana's *Nevermind* (1991). Some of the bands that rose to prominence during this period demonstrated a strong metal influence, and they often toured with metal bands in addition to mainstream rock acts. Consequently, the metal community loves these bands, and the mainstream community also loves these bands and is confused as to why the metal community loves these bands.

Alt-metal bands worth knowing include:

ALICE IN CHAINS, from Seattle. There's a clear Sabbath influence in its songs, all of which are written by guitarist Jerry Cantrell. Their lyrics are generally about heroin; the fact that original vocalist Layne Staley died from a heroin overdose in 2002 adds a chilling sheen of reality to the music. Staley is remembered for being one of the originators of the vocal style known as "yarling," which would become the most popular form of singing for moose-rock bands like Godsmack, Creed, and Nickelback.

FAITH NO MORE, from San Francisco. The only rule in Faith No More is, "There are no rules." Some of the band's songs, like "Jizzlobber" and "Surprise! You're Dead!," are undeniably metal. Other songs, like "Epic" and "Midlife Crisis," are mostly metal. And then songs like "Just a Man"

Alice In Chains but without buttons, California, August 1990.

and "Stripsearch" are not the least bit metal. One of its biggest hits was a very faithful cover of Lionel Richie's "Easy." The band recorded an original disco song ("Evidence"), an original country ballad ("Take This Bottle"), and an original polka song with German lyrics ("Das Schutzenfest"). FNM fans are cult-like in their devotion, treating charismatic, versatile vocalist Mike Patton as a deity.

LIVING COLOUR, an African-American quartet from New York City, was discovered by Mick Jagger while playing Manhattan's legendary CBGB's. The members of the band—guitarist Vernon Reid, vocalist Corey Glover, drummer Will Calhoun, and bassist Doug Wimbish—are considered musician's musicians, and in addition to metal, their music draws from prog, jazz, punk, blues, and other genres. You're familiar with the big-riffed single "Cult of Personality."

MELVINS are a proto-grunge band from Montesano, Washington. Frontman Buzz Osborne, known for his unique 'fro, went to high school with Kurt Cobain, and the Melvins were a clear influence on Nirvana. Many fans feel that if there were any justice in the world, the Melvins would have achieved a level of commercial success closer to that of Cobain and company. Despite never having gone quadruple platinum, the Melvins are revered, and also considered one of the progenitors of sludge metal.

MR. BUNGLE is the band from which Faith No More lifted vocalist Mike Patton after parting ways with original singer Chuck Mosley. Like FNM, Mr. Bungle plays experimental rock that indulges in any number of genres besides metal . . . but Mr. Bungle is even more extreme. FNM is a schizophrenic; Mr. Bungle is a schizophrenic who isn't on meds.

QUEENS OF THE STONE AGE rose from the ashes of the stoner-metal band Kyuss, from Palm Desert, California. True to those smoky roots, its sound may be best described as "fuzzy." Nirvana drummer Dave Grohl plays on the 2002 album *Songs for the Deaf*.

RAGE AGAINST THE MACHINE, from Los Angeles, is arguably the only band to ever successfully combine hip-hop with metal. As its name suggests, this is Noam Chomsky's favorite metal band. In addition to frontman Zack de la Rocha's sick flow, the band is known for Harvard-educated guitarist Tom Morello, who specializes in making weird sci-fi laser gun noises you wouldn't expect a guitar to be able to make.

SOUNDGARDEN, also from Seattle, answers the question, "What if Robert Plant had sung for Black Sabbath?" Although its sound became increasingly watered-down as its popularity grew, early albums like *Louder Than Love* (1989) and *Badmotorfinger* (1991) are not for the weak of heart.

TOOL, also from Los Angeles, is its generation's Pink Floyd: its music is proggy and moody and weird, and the band makes music videos that are like a more polished version of a Sarah Lawrence student's experimental thesis film, and you can get baked and study its album art for hours on end, and the musicians barely move onstage, but that's okay because they have an insanely cool laser show. Tool's following demonstrates a level of reverence that makes Faith No More fans seem tame by comparison; as a consequence, its concerts inspire a fervor that's almost religious in nature.

Extra Credit

1. ALICE IN CHAINS, "THEM BONES"
   (*Dirt*, 1992)

2. SOUNDGARDEN, "OUTSHINED"
   (*Badmotorfinger*, 1991)

3. FAITH NO MORE, "MIDLIFE CRISIS"
   (*Angel Dust*, 1992)

4. MELVINS, "HONEY BUCKET"
   (*Houdini*, 1993)

5. TOOL, "STINKFIST"
   (*Ænima*, 1996)

Mike Patton, metal's most dapper psychopath, in the early 1990s.

Drum Triggers: Trauma Triggers

Metal is no stranger to internal strife caused by divisive topics. Is it okay to listen to Burzum even though Varg Vikernes is a murdering bigot? What etiquette, if any, is applicable to moshing? Is Metallica's collaboration with Lou Reed, *Lulu* (2011), one of the worst records ever made, or *the* worst record ever made?

But perhaps no debate within the modern metal community is more heated than this: Is it or is it not okay to use drum triggers?

To answer this question, of course, we must first understand what a drum trigger actually is. In simplest terms, drum triggers are devices that one attaches to a drum kit to replace the natural sound of the drum with a different tone, which is provided by a hardware module or software plugin.

"A drum trigger acts like a microphone which, instead of miking up sounds through the air, picks up the vibration of a surface, so you just get a 'click' off of it," explains Nail the Mix's Eyal Levi. "So, normally, if you are miking up a snare and the drummer hits it, the sound travels through the air and into the microphone, which converts it into electricity, which goes into your recording gear and out comes the other end as the sound of a snare. But with a trigger, it's the same process except it's just picking up the actual hit on the drum head, and instead of taking that information and turning it into something we perceive as music, it just gives you the information of when the hit happened."

This hit, known as "the transient," then produces an artificial sound instead of the natural tone of the drum.

Although this may sound unnecessary, there's a very practical reason for the use of drum triggers, as Levi explains. "When the drummer is playing super-fast, as is often the case in metal, they don't have the time to stomp on the kick drum as hard as they would if they were playing slow. The time it takes to lift their foot or heel up and press it back down gets much shorter between each hit because you're at a higher BPM. Naturally, they're going to start playing more softly. That will make the bass drum sound muffled, quieter, and it will get lost. So it's advisable to use drum triggers for metal because the physics of playing very fast double-bass drums aren't very conducive to good sounds."

Drum triggers have been prevalent in metal since at least 1990, when Entombed used them on its classic album, *Left Hand Path*. Still, some detractors object to "unnatural" sound replacement, even though, as Levi explains, it's not very different from playing an electric guitar instead of an

acoustic one: "With an electric guitar, you pluck the string, and then the pick-up, through its weird magnet science, turns that into electricity, which then gets transferred into music. Drum triggers are no different from a pick-up or a microphone in that they're taking actual sound, converting it into electrical information, and outputting something else."

Levi also dismisses the argument that drum triggers allow drummers to "cheat," because they may not have to hit as hard or be as precise to achieve their desired sound as they would if they were simply playing acoustic drums. "If a drummer is really bad at double-bass and can't maintain a steady volume, drum triggers will help their dynamics. But if their timing sucks, it will not correct that. If the drummer is sloppy, it will just sound like really well defined slop. So in some ways, drum triggers expose bad playing."

Because triggers can be helpful or harmful depending on their user, Levi says he considers them to be "neutral," ultimately. "Triggers are a tool. You can use them or abuse them. If an airplane crashes because of pilot error, you don't recall all of those models of airplane. You can't blame the plane if the pilot flies it into the side of a mountain because he sucks at flying."

Former Entombed drummer Olle Dahlstedt did not play on *Left Hand Path*, but does use drum triggers, San Francisco, California, May 20, 2016.

5
Death Metal and Grindcore

WHAT IS IT?

Monsters banging pots and pans together.

WHO LISTENS TO IT?

People who watch slasher movies and root for the killer.

WHERE DOES IT COME FROM?

All over.

BASTARD CHILDREN:

Melodic death metal, blackened death metal, progressive death metal, technical death metal, blackened progressive melodic technical death metal, death 'n' roll, goregrind, electrogrind/cybergrind, pornogrind, powerviolence, slam metal.

THE BIG FOUR:

Death, Napalm Death, Carcass, Cannibal Corpse.

Death metal's only pretty face: Chuck Schuldiner of Death, New York City, February 1991.

In the '80s, some teenagers who loved thrash and/or hardcore punk decided to see just how far they could push those two forms of music. The answer, it turned out, was very, very far.

Possessed's 1985 debut, *Seven Churches*, is considered to be the first-ever death-metal album, with the group's vocalist/bassist, Jeff Becerra, credited with creating the term "death metal" itself. The San Francisco quartet sounds as though it was largely inspired by both NWOBHM and thrash bands . . . so long as those bands' members were on speed when they wrote the music, and walking over hot coals when they recorded it. Cronos from Venom had taken growling in metal vocals to new heights, but you could still understand what he was saying; Becerra sounds as though he'd been gargling with broken glass and battery acid.

Seven Churches definitely got the death-metal flaming car lined with explosives rolling, but it was really Florida's creatively named Death that detonated the movement in earnest.

The importance of Death—led by guitarist/vocalist Chuck Schuldiner—to the history of death metal cannot be overstated. The band's 1987 debut, *Scream Bloody Gore*, has many of the same characteristics as *Seven Churches*: guitars as sharp as any serrated blade, drums like cherry bombs going off inside your ears, leads so fast they leave flaming trail marks behind them, and vocals that sound like an overweight vampire howling as it's slowly fed into a meat grinder. But *Scream Bloody Gore* has two major advantages over Possessed's album: Schuldiner and incredible cover art by Ed Repka.

Schuldiner established himself as both a guitar god and a master composer from the get-go. Other

"This many churches minus three": Possessed at L'Amour in Brooklyn, New York, May 1987.

early death-metal bands wrote songs that were mostly plateaus—they were speedy but they never actually got anywhere. Schuldiner understood the inherent impact structure could provide. His songs had peaks and valleys, built and released tension.

As the years progressed, Schuldiner added more progressive and technical elements to Death's sound; the band's songs became increasingly esoteric, full of rhythms that constantly shift, and precise, discordant guitar solos. The second half of Death's discography sounds like a death-metal band that has studied and implemented jazz theory.

While bands like Repulsion, whose members Matt Olivo and Scott Carlson briefly flirted with joining Death, bludgeoned the listener, Death's attack was far more surgical. Consequently, Death was the key inspiration for the sub-subgenres of technical and progressive death metal. Performed by acts such as Gorguts, Atheist, Nile, Obscura, Origin, Necrophagist, and the Faceless, tech-death and prog-death bands basically make death metal that also goes to great pains to show off the members' proficiency with their instruments. Like latter-day Death, their lyrics also sometimes concern matters other than humans meeting their horrible ends, including philosophy, spirituality, and aliens.

Schuldiner would remain Death's only consistent member throughout its existence, but a substantial portion of the supporting characters who played with Death for a time almost all went on to become revered musicians in their own right—if they weren't already when they joined the band. They include Chris Reifert (Autopsy), Paul Masvidal and Sean Reinert (Cynic), Gene Hoglan (Dark Angel, Strapping Young Lad), Steve DiGiorgio (Testament), Richard Christy (Iced Earth), Andy LaRocque (King Diamond), and Terry Butler (Six Feet Under, Obituary). That so many gifted artists were all a part of Death at one time or another is a testament to both Schuldiner's eye for talent and his status within the metal community.

Following the release of *The Sound of Perseverance*, Schuldiner shifted his attention to a new band, Control Denied, a prog-metal project with nary a death-metal growl in sight. The band released its first and only album, *The Fragile Art of Existence*, in 1999. Schuldiner was working on a second Control Denied album when he passed away in 2001 from brain cancer. He remains one of metal's most influential and beloved figures to this day.

Deicide demonstrate their ambiguous feeilngs about Christianity at Milwaukee Metalfest, Wisconsin, 1990.

FEEL THE BURNS

Death's emergence in the late '80s paved the way for Florida's entire death-metal scene. While one might assume the Sunshine State became such an epicenter for death metal because musicians felt inspired by the swampy weather, overabundance of senior citizens living out their final days, and the unearthly horror that is Disney World, the reason was, in fact, far simpler.

"Everybody wanted to record at Morrisound,"

recalls Paul Mazurkiewicz, drummer for the legendary death metal band Cannibal Corpse. Located in Tampa, Morrisound Recording and its team of Jim Morris, Tom Morris, and, especially, Scott Burns, are nearly as famous as the musicians with whom they've worked.

"Scott was awesome," says Cannibal Corpse bassist Alex Webster. "As a producer, he was very focused on making sure we were locked in and playing tightly as a band. He heard things in our performances that needed improvement that we would have missed. We became a better band each time we recorded with him."

"How many death metal bands came to Tampa to work there?" Mazurkiewicz asks rhetorically. "They recorded with Death and Obituary and Deicide and Morbid Angel—some huge names in the death-metal genre."

Obituary's sound was more like a flail than a chainsaw: weighty, cumbersome, spinning, and lethal. Deicide was fronted by Glen Benton, an outspoken lightning rod for controversy whose list of accomplishments includes branding an inverted cross on his forehead and declaring that he would die at age thirty-three as Christ did (when Benton's thirty-third birthday came and went without his demise, some accused him of being a poseur). And Morbid Angel's vibe was pure Lovecraft; its song titles, album titles, album artwork, and logo design all invoked a nefarious religion's devious rituals. The band's lyrics even contained outright references to Lovecraft.

Up north, New York State birthed its own Unholy Trinity of death metal bands: Suffocation, from Long Island; Immolation, from Yonkers; and Buffalo's aforementioned Cannibal Corpse, who went on to become arguably the most successful death metal band of all time.

"It's hard for me to remember when I first heard 'death metal' used to describe a type of music," says Mazurkiewicz. "In the extreme/thrash/metal scene, the landscape was changing every few months, and we were living, growing with it. So we felt we were riding a wave of something new. We felt we were at the forefront of the emergence of this crazy kind of new music."

"It was definitely an exciting time," adds

Webster. "A lot of bands that had only been known in the tape trading/fanzine underground were getting signed to well-established independent metal labels. Then the bigger bands, like Morbid Angel and Death, started getting tour offers in Europe—prior to that, I think Possessed was the only American death-metal band that had toured Europe. It was clear something was going on, and we were excited to be a part of it."

In addition to making absolutely punishing music, Cannibal Corpse wrote the lyrical equivalent of nauseatingly explicit horror movies, screaming about "genital lacerating" and "brain turned to soup" (and that was just on one song, "Rotting Head").

Unsurprisingly, Cannibal Corpse has been the subject of some controversy over the years,

Morbid Angel at their most photogenic on Long Island, August 9, 1990.

condemned by conservative politicians like Bob Dole and banned in several countries. The band owes this honor not just to its lyrics but also to artist Vince Locke, who creates all of its album art and many of its merchandise designs. Locke's work is a perfect visual corollary to Cannibal Corpse's lyrics; for example, his cover for the group's 1992 album *Tomb of the Mutilated* depicts a female body that's been split down the middle receiving oral sex from the upper half of a zombie.

Anti–Cannibal Corpse authorities are badly

misguided, though. As is the case with many slasher-film franchises, the violence Cannibal Corpse portrays is so severe as to be absurd, like slapstick to the umpteenth degree. "We view what we do as horror entertainment, just like horror movies and novels," says Webster. "Death metal is a form of horror music. Just as horror filmmakers and novelists would not want to promote violence, neither do we."

One person who definitely understood Cannibal Corpse's work was a young Jim Carrey. The movie that launched Carrey's career,

1994's *Ace Ventura: Pet Detective*, includes a scene where the band performs its song "Hammer Smashed Face." Carrey personally went to great lengths to get the band into the movie, rearranging the shooting schedule to accommodate them.

"[Carrey] told us he owned some of our albums," Webster recalls, "and though when he first heard our music he thought it was extreme to the point of being ridiculous, it had actually grown on him." Carrey apparently even requested the specific song he wanted the band to play.

Despite their image, Cannibal Corpse's members are pussycats. Take, for example, second vocalist George "Corpsegrinder" Fisher, who replaced Chris Barnes in 1995. Onstage, the iconic, inhumanly thick-necked frontman does everything possible to earn his nickname, taunting the crowd when he feels it's not showing enough energy and headbanging with such intensity you'd think he was actively trying to detach his head from his body. But in real life, Fisher is a happily married family men who spends his free time dorking out over video games and RPGs.

Unlike its cousin, black metal, death metal doesn't spawn many actual murderers.

In any case, Mazurkiewicz believes the bands get the last laugh. "I think it's all ridiculous," the drummer says about the uproar. "We do our thing, we've been doing it for twenty-eight years . . . so these are minor speed bumps or roadblocks. But at the end of the day, people are talking about the band, and that's a good thing. Any publicity is good publicity."

The new Fab Four: Napalm Death, circa 1988.

SLAVES TO THE GRIND

Meanwhile, across the pond . . .

In 1981, adolescent Brits Nic Bullen, Miles "Rat" Ratledge, and Justin Broadrick united over a love of hardcore bands like Discharge and Siege. They weren't proficient musicians, but they didn't need to be for their purposes: if hardcore was punk on steroids, these kids were playing punk on steroids and painkillers and speed. The trio christened its band Napalm Death and created the form of extreme music that came to be known as "grindcore."

Grind offers the most extreme extremities available. It is the fastest, loudest, heaviest, craziest, most discordant, and often shortest form of music. Grind songs often last less than a minute, and any release featuring fewer than twenty songs yet lasting longer than half an hour might as well be a double album. Grindcore values grit, passion, and authenticity, arguably even more than other forms of extreme music. Performances don't have to be perfect, albums don't have to sound top-notch, and the best shows take place in firetrap squats in the middle of the day.

Pig Destroyer—arguably the finest grind band in the world today—may have created the ultimate grindcore mission statement with "Jennifer," the opening spoken-word track from its debut full-length, *Prowler in the Yard* (2001). Recited by a cold, computerized voice, "Jennifer" tells the story of two girls wrestling lasciviously in front of a public crowd, the onlookers "confused, or concerned, or shocked, or aroused, or all of the above." When a woman watching the scene while eating ice cream declares, "This is disgusting, it's pornography," a "balding professor type in his mid-forties, his left hand stuffed crassly down the front of his pants, [counters with] 'No, no, no. This is beautiful. This is art.'"

Is grindcore art, or is it shocking just for the sake of being shocking? This tension is the engine that powers grind. If you hear it and you're confused, that's because you're supposed to be, and if you don't "get it," then it's not for you anyway.

Napalm Death's music only became more extreme with the addition of drummer Mick Harris, who replaced Ratledge in 1985. Harris threw rhythm and nuance out the window altogether and concentrated on playing as fast as was humanly possible on his snare, bass drum, and cymbals simultaneously. The result came to be known as a "blast beat," which has become a staple of extreme music. Harris is also credited with creating the term "grindcore."

In 1987, Napalm Death released its debut full-length, *Scum*. On paper, *Scum* sounds completely ridiculous. But in your speakers, *Scum* sounds like an authentic burst of rage spat forth from the fringes of working class youth in Margaret Thatcher's UK.

Napalm Death, much closer to their classic lineup, Death in Spring Valley, New York, March 1991.

Scum is just as raw and relevant today as it was thirty years ago. It is notable not just for being the first proper grindcore album but for ensuring that grindcore, like hardcore, will never abandon its punk ideals. *Scum*'s lyrics and cover art are both overtly political; its songs are sometimes anarchistic simply for the sake of being anarchistic (one track, "You Suffer," is in the *Guinness Book of World Records* as the world's shortest song, somehow squeezing the phrase "You suffer but why?" into slightly more than a single second); and its DIY roots are on full display.

To wit: Harris is famously the only musician to play on the entire album, with the rest of the band's lineup changing from side A to side B of the record. Side A, recorded in 1986, was originally intended to be half of a split with another band (and only cost only £50.00 to produce). But by 1987, Bullen and Broadrick had both departed, and *Scum*'s side B was recorded with their replacements, Bill Steer (guitars), Jim Whitley (bass), and Lee Dorrian (vocals), who would go on to front legendary doom band Cathedral (see Doom Metal, page 177).

Napalm Death would continue to undergo lineup changes until its fourth album, 1992's *Utopia Banished*, with which it finally settled on a roster that would be maintained until 2006, when guitarist Jesse Pintado (also famous for his work with the grindcore band Terrorizer) passed away.

The band's other members, all of whom remain in Napalm Death to this day, are Barney Greenway (vocals), Shane Embury (bass), Mitch Harris (guitar, no relation to Mick), and Danny Herrera (drums). This definitive version of Napalm Death has been amazingly stable, remaining highly potent even now. Napalm Death is proof that a band can maintain its artistic integrity and continue to be successful for decades.

Needless to say, Napalm Death inspired scores of others grind bands. Prime examples include Extreme Noise Terror, Brutal Truth, Discordance Axis, Brujeria, Insect Warfare, Nasum, Gridlink, and Agoraphobic Nosebleed. Grind even sprouted its own sub-subgenres. Bands like Genghis Tron helped birth cybergrind by incorporating elements of electronic music; pornogrind, exemplified by bands like Gut, Cock and Ball Torture, and XXX Maniak, is a version of the form devoted entirely to sexual lyrics so explicit and filthy they'd make the Marquis de Sade blush; and powerviolence differentiates from grindcore in such a way that only super-duper-ultra-elite experts can possibly explain.

There are no rock stars in grindcore; the bands record and perform when they're able, and can often afford to remain creatively uncompromising because they don't earn their living from the music. Grindcore is the very personification of purity.

Carcass giving you bedroom eyes, Dallas, Texas, October 1990.

A HEALTHY CURIOSITY REGARDING THE HUMAN BODY

After 1988's *From Enslavement to Obliteration*, Bill Steer left Napalm Death to concentrate on Carcass, his band with drummer Ken Owen and bassist/vocalist Jeff Walker, who had created the album artwork for *Scum*.

Despite the association between the two bands, Carcass is a decidedly different beast from Napalm Death. For one thing, as you can probably guess from track titles like "Vomited Anal Tract" and "Fermenting Innards," Carcass is not political. More importantly, Carcass helped to create melodic death metal—a subgenre that's not quite as oxymoronic as one might assume.

As personified on albums like *Necroticism—Descanting the Insalubrious* (1991) and *Heartwork* (1993), Carcass's music at its best isn't just heavy and nefarious—it's cinematic, majestic, and catchy as flypaper. Or, put more simply: your mom will hate Carcass songs as much as she hates Napalm Death songs, but at least she'll recognize Carcass songs as songs.

But there can be too much of a good thing. In 1996, Carcass signed to a major label, Columbia, and recorded *Swansong*, an album many fans regard as being overly cutesy (the lead single was called "Keep on Rotting in the Free World") and

GMM 2008

unsatisfyingly poppy. That the band butted heads with Columbia and ultimately released the album through its original, far more metal-friendly label, Earache, probably did not help *Swansong*'s reception. *Swansong* thus ended up being pretty much the most accurate title imaginable: following its release, Carcass broke up for more than twenty years. The band reunited in 2008, and in 2013 released *Surgical Steel*, which was considered a return to form and a "true" follow-up to *Necroticism* and *Heartwork*.

Incidentally, Carcass also has the greatest song titles ever imagined. These include "Mucopurulence Excretor," "Empathological Necroticism," and "Lavaging Expectorate of Lysergide Composition." This band is responsible for more teenagers learning SAT words than Kaplan and the Princeton Review combined.

FUCK IKEA

It was Sweden, ultimately, that perfected melodeath. The country's initial, not-very-melodic death-metal scene included bands like Entombed, Grave, Dismember, Unleashed, and Dissection, who tuned their guitars way, way down and filtered them through various distortion pedals with their settings turned way up. The result was the creation of "buzzsaw guitars," so named because they sound like they can cut down redwoods.

Slaughter of the Soul

"GO!" At the Gates shredding Graspop, Belgium, 2008.

The tenor of the Swedish death-metal scene began to change in 1993, with Entombed's third release, *Wolverine Blues*. The album grafted death metal guitars and vocals onto the frames of more traditional, Motörhead-style hard-rock songs, resulting in "death 'n' roll." This new direction opened the door for death metal to take advantage of rock and even pop styles; like *Necroticism*, *Wolverine Blues* foreshadowed the arrival of Swedish melodeath.

That subgenre as we now know it arrived in the form of groups like Dark Tranquility, At the Gates, Soilwork, and In Flames, each of whom formed in or near the city of Gothenburg shortly before the release of *Necroticism*. Right around the time Carcass broke up, these bands were releasing the records that truly cemented melodeath's place in the metal establishment, doubling down on Carcass's sense of euphony and grandiosity to a fantastic end. Their impact on metal in the twenty-first century has been tremendous.

This is especially true of At the Gates' 1995 classic *Slaughter of the Soul*, which is a perfect melodeath album. Unlike its peers, however, At the Gates did not find much commercial success in the '90s—in fact, the band broke up less than a year after *Slaughter of the Soul*'s release. (Some of the band's members went on to find acclaim with other projects, including the Haunted, Disfear, and Lock Up.) Luckily, *Slaughter of the Soul* would come to be appreciated roughly a decade after it came out, thanks its clear influence on New Wave of American Heavy Metal bands including Darkest Hour and Killswitch Engage (see Metalcore, page 233). Like Carcass, At the Gates reformed after many years in 2008 and released an acclaimed reunion album, *At War with Reality*, in 2014.

The *machers* in Meshuggah, at Milwaukee Metalfest, Wisconsin, 1998.

FINALLY, A DEATH-METAL BAND YOUR BUBBE CAN APPRECIATE

Although Swedish metal is best known for its melodeath, its most singular export plays metal of an altogether different kind. Meshuggah, from Umeå, takes its name from the Hebrew word for "crazy."

The moniker is apt. Meshuggah's music is often polyrhythmic; for example, if drummer Tomas Haake is playing in a standard 4/4 time signature, guitarists Fredrik Thordendal and Mårten Hagström are likely playing in 17/16. It is also frequently polymetered, and the tempos change on a dime. The results are a Cubist jostling of death metal, prog, and jazz.

Musicians across all genres, understanding the complexity of Meshuggah's compositions and the level of skill it takes to perform their music, are the fastest to recognize the Swedes' brilliance.

For non-musicians, appreciating Meshuggah on anything other than an academic level may take some work . . . but the work is worth it. And, like At the Gates, Meshuggah would eventually spawn an entire movement almost single-handedly (see Deathcore and Djent, page 263). Meshuggah is about as close to a universally respected institution as metal has.

YOU CAN TEACH AN OLD ZOMBIE NEW TRICKS

While some bands continued to push death metal in new, increasingly melodic and technical directions, others began to boil the genre down to its bare essentials. Bands like Internal Bleeding and Pyrexia sounded as though they'd listened to Suffocation and decided that shit was just too complicated. They piled breakdowns upon breakdowns and somehow managed to make death metal vocals even less intelligible, ostensibly offering gurgles that imitate Montezuma's Revenge. This form of death metal took on the apropos name "slam."

Dying Fetus, from Maryland, represents slam's pinnacle. Its music slams harder than a skydiver with a defective parachute. What sets Dying Fetus apart from other slam bands is its members, talent as songwriters; the riffs on their third album, 2000's *Destroy the Opposition*, latch onto the memory like a parasite, demanding repeat listens. Dying Fetus is fun to listen to even when you're not moshing with concussion-inducing force.

Today, death metal and grindcore continue to develop. Acts like the Black Dahlia Murder and Arsis fly the flag for traditional death metal, while groups such as Fuck the Facts, Magrudergrind, Wormrot, and Maruta keep the grindcore nightmare alive.

But some bands, including Misery Index, Cattle Decapitation, and Cephalic Carnage, have amalgamated the genres. For these groups, the line between death and grind is invisible. This is probably very convenient for your mom, who can't tell Brutal Truth from Bolt Thrower anyway.

Bolt Thrower taking a break from painting Warhammer figurines, November 1991.

Starter Kit

Ready to bleed?
You will need . . .

- ☐ LONG-SLEEVE T-SHIRT WITH ILLEGIBLE BAND LOGO, BLACK
- ☐ CARGO SHORTS, BLACK OR CAMO
- ☐ LOW-TOP SNEAKERS, BLACK
- ☐ CHAIN WALLET
- ☐ *FACES OF DEATH* VHS TAPE
- ☐ SUBSCRIPTION TO *WORLD OF WARCRAFT*
- ☐ PIZZA PIE, LARGE
- ☐ MOUNTAIN DEW, 2 LT. BOTTLE
- ☐ PEPTO-BISMOL, 8 OZ.
- ☐ DEODORANT, 0 OZ.

Homework

1. POSSESSED, "PENTAGRAM"
(Seven Churches, 1985)

2. DEATH, "SPIRITUAL HEALING"
(Spiritual Healing, 1990)

3. OBITUARY, "INTERNAL BLEEDING"
(Slowly We Rot, 1989)

4. MORBID ANGEL, "IMMORTAL RITES"
(Altars of Madness, 1989)

5. REPULSION, "DRIVEN TO INSANITY"
(Horrified, 1989)

6. DEICIDE, "DEAD BY DAWN"
(Deicide, 1990)

7. ENTOMBED, "LEFT HAND PATH"
(Left Hand Path, 1990)

8. SUFFOCATION, "INFECTING THE CRYPTS"
(Effigy of the Forgotten, 1991)

9. CARCASS, "CORPORAL JIGSAW QUANDRY"
(Necroticism--Descanting the Insalubrious, 1991)

10. IMMOLATION, "THOSE LEFT BEHIND"
(Dawn of Possession, 1991)

11. BOLT THROWER, "WHAT DWELLS WITH"
(War Master, 1991)

12. ENTOMBED, "TWISTED MASS OF BURNT DECAY"
(Mental Funeral, 1991)

13. CANNIBAL CORPSE, "HAMMER SMASHED FACE"
(Tomb of the Mutilated, 1992)

14. GORGUTS, "THE EROSION OF SANITY"
(The Erosion of Sanity, 1993)

15. AT THE GATES, "SLAUGHTER OF THE SOUL"
(Slaughter of the Soul, 1995)

16. MESHUGGAH, "FUTURE BREED MACHINE"
(Destroy Erase Improve, 1995)

17. CRYPTOPSY, "GRAVES OF THE FATHERS"
(None So Vile, 1996)

18. DYING FETUS, "PRAISE THE LORD (OPIUM OF THE MASSES)"
(Destroy the Opposition, 2000)

19. IN FLAMES, "BULLET RIDE"
(Clayman, 2000)

20. CHILDREN OF BODOM, "SIXPOUNDER"
(Hate Crew Deathroll, 2003)

21. NILE, "MASTURBATING THE WAR GOD"
(Black Seeds of Vengeance, 2000)

22. DECAPITATED, "SPHERES OF MADNESS"
(Nihility, 2002)

23. NECROPHAGIST, "STABWOUND"
(Epitaph, 2004)

24. THE BLACK DAHLIA MURDER, "I'M CHARMING"
(Miasma, 2005)

25. THE FACELESS, "ANCIENT COVENANT"
(Planetary Duality, 2008)

26. EXTREME NOISE TERROR, "WE THE HELPLESS"
(A Holocaust in Your Head, 1989)

27. NAPALM DEATH, "SUFFER THE CHILDREN"
(Harmony Corruption, 1990)

28. BRUTAL TRUTH, "DENIAL OF EXISTENCE"
(Extreme Conditions Demand Extreme Responses, 1994)

29. PIG DESTROYER, "PISS ANGEL"
(Prowler in the Yard, 2001)

30. AGORAPHOBIC NOSEBLEED, "KILL THEME FOR AMERICAN APESHIT"
(Frozen Corpse Stuffed with Dope, 2002)

Death at the "Combat Revenge" video shoot, at the Trocadero, Philadelphia, Pennsylvania. We miss you, Chuck.

Glenn Danzig sweaty from moving his **MOTHER FUCKING BRICKS**, the Netherlands, 1993. If you don't get it, look it up.

A Crash Course in Goth Metal

For modern fans, "goth" can mean anything from the monotone minimalism of Bauhaus to the spunky dance metal of Coal Chamber. But as a specific musical style, goth metal focuses on the slow and depressive—the bass is thick, the guitars are fuzzy, the drums have a lot of reverb, and the vocals are grumbled, crooned, and wept. While variations exist, this lush and shadowy sound is the grave dirt in which goth metal sleeps. Like a vampire? Like a vampire.

The most influential goth metal musician is surely Glenn Danzig. As the lead singer of horror punk originators the Misfits, Danzig incorporated Elvis Presley–like wails into tracks about movie monsters while decked out in greasepaint eyeliner, skeleton-print clothes, and emphasized widow's peaks dubbed "Devillocks" (Metallica bassist Cliff Burton was famously a huge fan). But it was with his hardcore band Samhain, and his following solo career, that Danzig put goth metal on the map, whooping over countrified rock music and showing off his pecs while humorlessly reciting *Paradise Lost*. The song "Mother," from his Rick Rubin–produced debut album, is the quintessential metal karaoke track.

Three bands from England—Paradise Lost, My Dying Bride, and Akercocke—added goth overtones to extreme music with mixed results. Paradise Lost was the most listenable of the three, borrowing heaps of melody from its Scandinavian brethren. My Dying Bride went off the gloomy deep end with swooning

Tears for fears: HIM, June 1999.

watching a Dra
movie and pro
the indulgent
occultism cha
by the "wicke
man in all of E
Aleister Crow

Gothic pow
metal act Nigh
was the most
popular band
underground f
time, its baroq
songs about fa
highlighted by
voice of singer
Turunen, who
headlines in t
band's native
when she was
in 2005. Easil
most popular f
fronted goth m
band is Italy's
Coil, led by rav
haired singer
Scabbia, a tale
and dynamic v
known by man
Revolver maga
"Hottest Chick
Metal." Lacun

dirges about committing suicide over ladies.
Akercocke merged brutal death metal with
classic British sensibilities, displayed outwardly
by the band members wearing three-piece
suits. Its music sounds like Morbid Angel

continues to be one of metal's best-selling
bands, inspiring countless imitators like I
Moment, Within Temptation, and Amaran
For all its melodramatic darkness,

HELLRAISERS

goth metal sells surprisingly well when it's easily digestible. Finland's HIM (its name an acronym for a misheard Deicide lyric, "His Infernal Majesty") rose to massive mainstream recognition on a surging wave of chocolaty guitars and the heartbroken croon of hypersexual alcoholic Ville Valo. The band's biggest release was 2003's *Love Metal*, the cover of which features a Heartagram, HIM's official symbol, which combines, you guessed it, a heart and a pentagram, and which would end up tattooed on members of metalcore bands like Killswitch Engage and Bleeding Through. More recently, Sweden's Ghost has taken the world by storm with spooky doom that sounds like Mercyful Fate Lite. The band is fronted by the skull-faced anti-pope Papa Emeritus, with a backing band of "Nameless Ghouls" in Venetian opera masks. Its music is cinematic and catchy, and its third album, *Meliora*, won a Grammy in 2016.

But no goth metal band has ever been as successful, talented, or truly miserable as Type O Negative. Led by Peter Steele, the statuesque former frontman for barbarian thrashers Carnivore, Type O embraced and escaped every goth cliché. Though the music was deeply depressed, the dudes behind it were known for their self-deprecating senses of humor. The band never wore lace or vinyl but instead dressed in blue-collar clothes in their signature dirty-penny green. Steele spoke in a heavy Brooklyn accent but only used it in songs to emphasize what a blunt instrument he truly was; though a towering figure known for his withering scowl, he posed for *Playgirl* in 1995, then wrote an upbeat song called "I Like Goils"

about how much he hated it when gay men asked him to sign the issue. The band never released a bad album but understandably broke up when Steele died tragically of heart failure in 2010.

Goth metal continues to alienate and depress, be it in the form of polished core kids like Motionless in White or sewer sweethearts like Beastmilk. But one thing's certain: as long as love-struck young people feel bad about how things turned out, goth metal will always be there, thumping softly out of a window with an incense burner on the sill.

Extra Credit

1. DANZIG, "HER BLACK WINGS"
(*II: Lucifuge*, 1990)

2. PARADISE LOST, "SAY JUST WORDS"
(*One Second*, 1997)

3. LACUNA COIL, "HEAVEN'S A LIE"
(*Comalies*, 2002)

4. HIM, "RIGHT HERE IN MY ARMS"
(*Razorblade Romance*, 1999)

5. TYPE O NEGATIVE, "BLACK NO. 1 (LITTLE MISS SCARE-ALL)"
(*Bloody Kisses*, 1993)

6. GHOST, "SQUARE HAMMER"
(*Popestar EP*, 2016)

Black Metal

WHAT IS IT?

A more atmospheric form of death metal, with stronger political/philosophical inclinations, less traditional structure, and shittier production, as performed by dudes in clown makeup.

WHO LISTENS TO IT?

Catholic school rejects, people who wish death-metal musicians were actually murderers, hipsters from Brooklyn and Portland.

WHERE DOES IT COME FROM?

Scandinavia.

BASTARD CHILDREN:

Symphonic black metal, National Socialist black metal (NSBM), war metal, blackgaze, unblack metal (a.k.a. "Christian black metal").

THE BIG FOUR:

Enslaved, Emperor, Darkthrone, Mayhem.

Truly terrifying: Bathory's Quorthon, circa 1987.

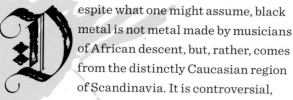

Despite what one might assume, black metal is not metal made by musicians of African descent, but, rather, comes from the distinctly Caucasian region of Scandinavia. It is controversial, at odds with Christianity, and so humorless as to be hilarious (adorning oneself in allegedly scary clown makeup known as "corpse paint" is a common practice in black metal). And yet it's critically revered, even by mainstream media outlets.

The first reason for this is, naturally, that black metal can be great.

The second reason for this is that black metal is to extreme music as gangsta rap is to hip-hop. Death-metal bands sing about violence, but in the genre's heyday, black-metal bands practiced it.

HUMOR: IT'S NOT FOR EVERYONE

The bands referred to as the "first wave" of black metal rose to prominence in the '80s, but the music of those groups is not really black metal as we've come to think of it today.

Take, for example, Venom. Its 1982 album, *Black Metal*, gave the genre its name, and the band certainly pushed Satanism in metal to new extremes. Musically, however, Venom has more in common with Iron Maiden than it does with Immortal (see NWOBHM, page 39).

Likewise, corpse paint is derived from the black-and-white makeup worn by Mercyful Fate's King Diamond . . . but no black metal vocalist actually sounds like King Diamond, who sings at a frequency only audible to dogs.

Celtic Frost (see Thrash Metal, page 93) is sometimes deemed black metal because its members were Swiss, used satanic imagery and Wagnerian horn sections, wore makeup, referenced brisk weather, and never smiled. But their music was too tight, and its connection to old school rock 'n' roll music too readily apparent, to be black metal.

Sweden's Bathory has the most legitimate claim to being the first black-metal band. Its music focused on capital-*E* Evil and Scandinavian history and seemed unpracticed and untreated, powered by concussive, unrelenting drums and a wall of guitars, with seemingly every setting on its amps turned up to eleven. Furthermore, Bathory's mastermind, Tomas Forsberg, performed under the stage name "Quorthon," which has a nice Lovecraftian ring to it but doesn't actually mean anything. "Quorthon" has been the model for all stage names in black metal ever since.

The first honest-to-Satan black metal bands, however, came out of Norway, long after Bathory's career had begun and Mercyful Fate had broken up.

In 1991, twenty-three-year-old Øystein "Euronymous" Aarseth opened a metal record store in Oslo called Helvete ("Hell"). The store became the headquarters for the Svarte Sirkel ("The Black Circle"), an insular club containing the men who created black metal as we now know it. Besides Euronymous, other fancifully monikered members of Svarte Sirkel included his Mayhem bandmates Dead, Necrobutcher, and Hellhammer; Emperor's Ihsahn, Samoth, and Faust; Darkthrone's Fenriz and Nocturno Culto; and Burzum's Varg Vikernes (a.k.a. Count Grishnackh, though we feel that "Varg" is stage name enough).

The members of Svarte Sirkel didn't see metal simply as a form of music but as a way of life. They sought to end Christianity and were obsessed with who was "true" (later bastardized on the Internet

Quorthon and friend.

Take it from Mirai Kawashima, frontman and general mastermind for the acclaimed Tokyo black metal band Sigh, which was once signed to the Euronymous-owned indie label, Deathlike Silence Records. "Black metal was a resurrection of good old thrash metal from the '80s," Kawashima explains. "You know, things were totally different in the early '90s. Now all the extreme metal subgenres co-exist, but back then, death metal and grindcore were almost killing thrash metal. People thought that death metal was the superior version of thrash metal, and thrash metal was considered to be something totally outdated. The first question you got [about your band] was, 'How many semitones do you downtune?' And some people could not keep up with the pace [of the ever-changing trends]." Black metal, Kawashima asserts, was intended to walk everything back a step or two. "Extreme metal kept evolving towards the end of the '80s. NWOBHM became thrash metal and thrash metal became death metal. But in the early '90s, extreme metal looked back at the past for the first time. Death metal was born by looking to the future. But black metal was born through nostalgia."

as "tr00," meaning an authentic metal fan) and who was "false" (meaning a poseur). As Morgan "Evil" Håkansson, guitarist for the celebrated Swedish black metal band Marduk, told *MetalSucks* in 2013, "Satanic beliefs and a dedication to that cause: that's what makes you 'black metal.'"

This militancy extended to all aspects of Svarte Sirkel's worldview, and today, the bands are equally well known for their ideology as they are for their sound.

Musically, black metal differentiated itself via Euronymous's employment of three-note open guitar chords instead of the two-note power chords more traditionally utilized in metal. It made the music feel looser, ghostlier, and more chaotic than other metallic genres. Furthermore, black metal's vocal style is more of phlegm-saturated croak than a death-metal scream. To the uneducated ear, these differences may seem insignificant. In fact, they're anything but; the deliberate sloppiness is meant to invoke devolution.

Have it Norway: Mayhem at Roskilde, Denmark, 1991.

The best examples of Norwegian black metal remain the seminal albums the members of Svarte Sirkel released in 1994. Darkthrone's *Transilvanian Hunger* sounds like it was recorded through a wall of maggots inside of a prolapsed anus; it's so raw one feels in danger of getting trichinosis just listening to it. Emperor's *In the Nightside Eclipse* added a sense of majesty to black metal by giving the songs a progressive bent and elements of classical music, which Emperor's members claimed was the only thing they listened to. And then there's Mayhem's *De Mysteriis Dom Sathanas* ("About the Mystery of the Lord Satan"), which is bleakly ethereal and full of lyrics about pagans and the dark and the past and the dark past of the pagans.

These lyrics, written by Dead, demonstrated an obsession with the pre-Christian past and heavily emphasized the act of returning—to nature, Paganism, and the allegedly innate order of things. They're nationalistic, sentimental, and conservative.

Which helps explain all the violence.

LIVE FAST, DIE YOUNG, TAKE PHOTOS OF THE CORPSE

Predictably, Dead was the first to go. His lyrics may appear on *De Mysteriis Dom Sathanas*, but his voice never does. By the time that album came out, it had been more than three years since he'd taken his own life and been replaced by Attila Csihar.

Euronymous found Dead's body in an apartment they shared, along with a suicide note that began, "Excuse the blood, but I have slit my wrists and neck." He did not, however, apologize for the additional gore caused by shooting himself with a shotgun.

Euronymous's reaction upon discovering his friend's body was not to contact the authorities, but rather to go purchase a camera, take photographs of the gory scene, and gather skull fragments. The photo eventually became the cover of Mayhem's 1998 live album, *Dawn of the Black Hearts*, while the skull fragments were turned into necklaces awarded to those Euronymous deemed "true."

Dead popularized corpse paint. His aim was to literally look like a corpse, and he'd even bury

This fucking dipshit (Varg Vikernes, neo-Nazi murderer).

his clothes in the ground prior to shows to emulate a lifeless body's stench. He survived a near-death experience as a child, was frequently depressed, often mutilated himself while performing (in addition to using real animal carcasses as stage props—a practice shared by Gorgoroth), and may have had Cotard delusion, a mental illness in which the victim believes himself to be a walking corpse. It's clear that he was obsessed with death as well as with black metal dogma. He may have viewed his suicide as the ultimate "true" act, proof that his morose demeanor was not just for show; that he was credible and devoted to the cause.

Dead's suicide put Norwegian black metal on the map. Necrobutcher subsequently left Mayhem as a result of Euronymous's actions, accusing the guitarist of exploiting Dead's tragic end for fame; he was subsequently replaced by the aforementioned Varg Vikernes, who appears on *Mysteriis*.

Which is when shit got really nuts.

Besides their love of music, Euronymous and Vikernes bonded over their subscription to right-wing doctrine. Writing to a fan in '92, Euronymous professed admiration for Stalin, Ceausescu, and Pol Pot, while Vikernes claimed that "shooting N*ggers, Jews, and the Like should be fucking Rewarded."

But by 1993, Vikernes felt Euronymous was getting too much credit for the burgeoning black-metal scene. Euronymous boasted about his exploits to fans and friends, instructing Kawashima not to discuss Svarte Sirkel on the phone because he thought INTERPOL might be listening in. But in a letter to a fan, Vikernes claimed that "Only ME and two of the guys in EMPEROR have been practising what we preach. NOBODY ELSE."

That summer, Vikernes went over to Euronymous's home, allegedly to discuss some money that was owed to him by Deathlike Silence. Then Vikernes stabbed Euronymous twenty-three times, sixteen instances of which were in the back. He later claimed he'd acted in self-defense.

The court didn't buy it. In May of 1994, Vikernes was sentenced to twenty-one years in prison, convicted of murder as well as multiple church burnings and possession of explosives.

Vikernes produced several Burzum albums while in prison, but the Norwegian penal system is not known for its recording facilities, and these albums make *Transilvanian Hunger*'s production seem slick. They're also roughly as exciting as watching mold grow. Still, they're considered brilliant by people who don't want to admit that they themselves are bigots.

Vikernes was released on parole in 2009 and relocated to France with his wife and children, where he continued to spread his intolerant philosophy via a series of blogs and videos. In 2013, he was arrested and convicted by French authorities for attempting to incite racial hatred against Jews and Muslims. He was sentenced to six months probation and forced to pay a fine of €8,000. Still, Vikernes continues to make videos about the alleged benefits of racial segregation, as well as tabletop RPGs about how valiant the Norse people were before diversity came along and ruined everything.

Following the murder of Euronymous and conviction of Vikernes, Necrobutcher rejoined Mayhem. The band continues to this day, despite, or perhaps because of, their dark past.

Emperor pouring baroque magma onto the Inferno Festival, Oslo, Norway, April 2006.

JESUS HAD GREAT ABS

Vikernes was not the only member of Svarte Sirkel to be convicted of arson or murder. In fact, the church burnings for which Vikernes was convicted were only four of fifty committed in Norway between 1992 and 1996, all of which destroyed historical landmarks nearly as old as Christianity itself. Other Norwegian black-metal musicians who were eventually arrested and sentenced for participation in these acts of arson include Emperor's Samoth and Faust.

Additionally, Faust was convicted for killing Magne Andreassen, a gay man, in the woods near Lillehammer. According to Faust, Andreassen propositioned him while he was walking through a park; Faust pretended to be interested, followed Andreassen to the forest, and stabbed him thirty-seven times. Faust did not claim his crime was an act of self-defense, and in 1994 he was sentenced to fourteen years in jail. He was released for good behavior in 2003; in 2014, he briefly rejoined Emperor for special performances celebrating the twentieth anniversary of *In the Nightside Eclipse*'s release. Samoth served sixteen months in prison before rejoining Emperor.

The other participants in Svarte Sirkel never committed crimes as heinous as the members of Mayhem and Emperor, but they did certainly have their brushes with controversy and morally questionable decisions.

Take, for example, a 1995 interview with Gorgoroth's then-vocalist, Kristian "Gaahl" Espedal. During the course of the discussion, which was conducted by the tastefully named *Polish Holocaust* 'zine, Gaahl used a plethora of racial slurs, while expressing positive opinions

Inspiration for *The Baby-Sitter's Club*. Gorgoroth, backstage at Wacken Festival, Germany, in 1999.

Transilvanian Hunger

about Vikernes and Hitler. But in a 2008 interview with *Rock Hard*, while discussing being an openly gay man in the predominantly hetero black metal arena, Gaahl recanted his comments, claiming, "There have definitely been changes and an evolution in my thinking."

Darkthrone, meanwhile, ran into trouble because *Transilvanian Hunger*, which included lyrics written by Vikernes, arrived with a statement asserting, "If any man should attempt to criticize this LP, he should be thoroughly patronized for his obviously Jewish behavior." The band soon released this semi-atonement:

> **Darkthrone can only apologize for this tragic choice of words. In Norway the word "Jew" is used all the time to mean something that is out of order. If something breaks down, if something is stupid, etc. . . . When we wrote "Jewish behavior" in our previous press statement, we could have easily have [sic] written, according to the Norwegian language "stupid" instead.**

The band also included a message in its 1995 album, *Panzerfaust*, insisting, "Darkthrone is certainly not a Nazi band nor a political band. Those of you who still might think so, you can lick Mother Mary's asshole in eternity." Although that did not explain why *Panzerfaust* took its name from a Nazi weapon, for most fans this declaration, and the fact that the band hasn't been accused of any intolerant behavior since, has been enough to let them off the hook.

Darkthrone remains popular today, and the always-quirky Fenriz has become a special source of fascination for black metal fans: he's worked in the Norwegian postal industry for nearly thirty

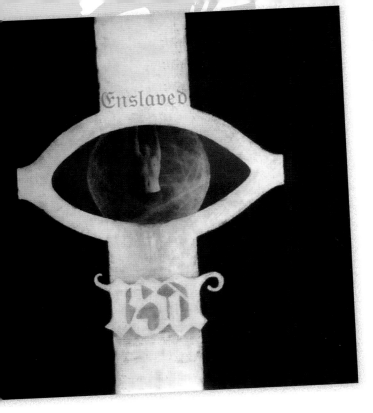

years, sorting and coding letters, and, in 2016, he was elected to his local town council in Kolbotn . . . despite his campaign poster featuring a photograph of him holding his cat and the slogan "Please Don't Vote for Me."

MORAL DILEMMA NOT REQUIRED

Not all Norwegian black metal bands are populated by pricks. Mayhem and Emperor had plenty of peers that have managed to steer clear of any such misdeeds, including Immortal, Ulver, Carpathian Forest, Satyricon, 1349, and Dimmu Borgir.

In fact, in a 2014 interview, Ivar Bjørnson, Enslaved's guitarist and co-mastermind (alongside bassist/screamer Grutle Kjellson), specifically denounced such small-minded views, asserting, "Paganism is beyond segregation." That the members of Enslaved are not bigoted dickheads comes as a great relief: in black-metal circles, the band is considered next-level brilliant.

It's easy to understand why. Enslaved has released thirteen albums in twenty-one years, and its creative evolution has been remarkable. Though 1994's *Frost* sounds similar to the other Norwegian black-metal records released that year, the group began to expand its palate on 1997's *Eld*, which includes soaring, otherworldly vocals in addition to the usual throaty black-metal barks, and characteristically ferocious sections balanced out by long, dreamy, often instrumental passages.

By the time Enslaved made *Isa*, ten years after *Frost*, the band had added keyboardist and clean vocalist Herbrand Larsen to its lineup, resulting in its most multifaceted work to date. Larsen's style of singing is forlorn and borderline inexpressive, the vocal equivalent of the thousand-yard stare, while his synths brought a distinctly psychedelic flavor to the band's already increasingly proggy symphonies. Enslaved's songs describe Norwegian history and folklore but don't do so in a way that suggests longing for the past so much as a search for larger metaphysical meaning. For example, on the track "Veilburner," from 2012's brilliant *RIITIIR*, the lyrics confront one of life's most painful realities ("Finding the truth doesn't mean there's an answer") before appropriating the metaphor of Plato's cave ("I can not tolerate being held in the dark / I need to see").

The contrast between the frothing howls of Kjellson and the haunted melodies of Larsen feels bittersweet. It's interesting to note that while there is no shortage of bands that clearly model themselves on Gorgoroth and Darkthrone, few dare to follow in Enslaved's ambitious footsteps. The group is one of a kind.

Dimmu Borgir borgettin' down, Highbury Garage, London, 1997.

LEND ME YOUR BORGIRS

The biggest black-metal band of all time, at least in terms of records sold, is Norway's Dimmu Borgir. The band formed in 1993, and it's safe to assume that its founding members—vocalist Shagrath, guitarist Silenoz, and drummer Tjodalv—looked up to the Svarte Sirkel. As time went on, however, Dimmu Borgir became increasingly bold in its use of synthesizers and melody, pushing their use in black metal far beyond anything Emperor had ever attempted. The band was soon deemed "symphonic black metal."

Dimmu Borgir's best records, 2001's *Puritanical Euphoric Misanthropia* and 2003's *Death Cult Armageddon*, truly are like symphonies, chock full of musical peaks and valleys but not breaks. Furthermore, both albums were recorded not with synthesizers but with actual orchestras. There's plenty of aggression to go around on these releases, but there are also instrumental tracks like *Misanthropia*'s "Fear and Wonder" and "Perfection or Vanity," which sound like the scores to major Hollywood films. In fact, "Progenies of the Great Apocalypse" and "Eradication Instincts Defined," the hit singles from *Death Cult Armageddon*, were used to great effect in the promotional campaign for Guillermo Del Toro's horror/action film *Hellboy*.

Surely, it is also not a coincidence that both of these albums were made with Dimmu Borgir's strongest lineup—including Arcturus's I.C.S. Vortex on bass and clean vocals, former Cradle of Filth drummer Nicholas Barker, and, perhaps most importantly, keyboardist Mustis, who wrote the records' grand orchestral parts.

Following the release of 2007's *In Sorte Diaboli*, those three members of the band were fired under mysterious circumstances, with Mustis claiming that he was let go via a text that read, simply, "Goodbye." Regardless, Dimmu Borgir remains wildly popular, if largely considered un-"true."

SOME IMPROVEMENTS ARE GOOD, HOWEVER

Given Kawashima's own admission that black metal is a genre rooted in nostalgia, it is ironic that Sigh would go on to become one of black metal's most forward-thinking and experimental bands. Starting with their fifth full-length, 2001's *Imaginary Sonicscapes*, the band basically went batshit crazy (in the best possible way). The album's title could not be more appropriate. It is the *Brown Acid* of black metal. It has wavy synths and female back-up singers and bluesy guitar solos and Ennio Morricone–esque orchestral sections and all other manner of delightful insanity. Some albums seem experimental when they're released, but are imitated to the point of seeming fairly normal with the passage of time; Sigh's discography from *Imaginary Sonicscapes* onward was, is, and always will be really, really fucking weird.

The band's willingness to experiment may have arisen from the fact that they never really "belonged" in the first place. At the time of their formation, Sigh weren't part of a larger Japanese black metal scene; they were the Japanese black metal scene. "Seriously, EVERYBODY was enthusiastic about death metal, grindcore, Earache, downtuning, etc.," says Kawashima. The only other person Kawashima knew who "still appreciated the older evil bands" was Yasuyuki Suzuki, vocalist, guitarist, and bassist for the band Abigail. "There was only Abigail and Sigh [playing black metal in Japan], nobody else in the early days." As you can imagine, this had an alienating effect on the band. "I didn't feel as though we were at the forefront of a new genre," Kawashima admits. "We were more the outcasts of the scene than [a band] leading a new scene."

Regardless of their reasons, the band's willingness to disregard the rules of traditional black metal is the reason their name is now written in the annals of metal history (in blood, natch). "Obviously, when we did *Imaginary Sonicscape* in 2001, we wanted to move away from 'traditional black metal' image," Kawashima concedes. "Back then, here in Japan, so many young black metal bands came out of nowhere, and they all looked and sounded the same. We didn't want to be a part of that.

"I just wanted to mix extreme metal with the atmosphere of horror movies," Kawashima continues. "I realized that twentieth century classical music was often used in horror soundtracks. Then I started studying the composition technique of twentieth century classical music, which happened to be experimental.

"The fact that I myself am a keyboardist/pianist was the key. If I were a guitarist, Sigh's music would probably be quite different. Guitars are usually used as guitars, but keyboards are often used as a substitute for many other instruments—strings, brass, or even a human choir. In that sense, being a keyboardist can be the key to being eclectic about music."

Sigh release a new album every two to three years like clockwork, each as odd, fascinating, and just plain rocking as the last. They are one of the last truly unpredictable creative forces in metal. May they never change.

THERE'S NO SUCH THING AS BAD PUBLICITY.

Despite traveling beyond Norway, controversy still seems to follow black metal wherever it goes. In most cases, that controversy stems from black metal's ongoing assault on Christianity.

The band to make the most headlines in mainstream media outlets as a result of its anti-Christian stance is undoubtedly Cradle of Filth, from England. In 1993, the group released a shirt adorned with an image of a masturbating nun along with the phrases "Vestal Masturbation" and "Jesus Is a Cunt." In countries where insulting Christianity is a crime, fans caught wearing the shirt were arrested and prosecuted; in more lenient countries, kids just got expelled from school. As recently as 2015, a New Zealand woman desecrated one of these shirts while it was on display at a museum. *Rolling Stone* magazine consequently named the merch item "the most controversial shirt in rock history."

It's fair to say that the shirt is now more famous than the band . . . which some black metal fans would consider to be a good thing. "Tr00 kvltists" generally look down their noses at Cradle of Filth for ostensibly being the Disneyland version of a black-metal band. The music is flowery, the band's iterations of corpse paint owe as much to glam as to King Diamond, its stage shows often feature circus performers, and its music tends to have an Anne Rice vibe to it. Sure, it's evil, but it's a romanticized evil. The band's biggest hit, "Nymphetamine," is a duet between diminutive frontman Dani Filth and Liv Kristine of symphonic metal band Leaves Eyes, and features lyrics like "This lust, a vampyric addiction / To her alone in full submission." For

Dani Filth, presumably standing on a phone book, circa the late '90s by the looks of those rings.

Behemoth backstage in Randolph, New Jersey, 2003.

some, Cradle of Filth is too much Dracula, not enough Lucifer. The band seems unphased by these criticisms, however—likely because it sells a shit ton of records.

Far better respected and almost as incendiary is Behemoth. Led by charismatic guitarist/vocalist Adam "Nergal" Darski, the Polish band specializes in a more muscular, militaristic form of black metal often referred to as "blackened death metal" ("death-y black metal" might be more accurate, but it doesn't quite roll off the bifurcated tongue the same way). In his native country, Nergal's a bona-fide rock star who has dated mainstream pop starlets, been on the cover of *Newsweek*, and acted as a judge for the reality singing program *The Voice*. Thus, Nergal's conflicts with religious authorities tend to be a pretty big deal.

To wit: during a 2007 concert in Gdynia, Nergal called the Catholic Church "the most murderous cult on the planet" before destroying a copy of the Bible, which he deemed "a book of lies." All in a night's work for your average black metal musician . . . except, in Poland, insulting religion is a crime. A Catholic group sued Nergal, and in 2012 Poland's Supreme Court ruled against him. Although the frontman was able to avoid a possible two-year prison sentence for his "crime," Behemoth was banned from playing the city of Poznań. In 2014, Russian immigration officials detained the entire band mid-tour, alleging its members lacked the proper paperwork, despite having entered the country on business visas. After spending a night in jail, they were deported back to Poland. It is suspected that they were made to jump through these hoops as retaliation for being anti-Christian.

What these religious figures don't seem to understand is that every time they try to ban or arrest a black-metal band, they are actually helping them to make fans. Telling adolescents that something is forbidden is the fastest way to ensure that they try it.

Motherf— wait, that's not Richard Spencer, it's George Clarke of Deafheaven playing the Pitchfork Music Festival, Chicago, 2014.

OR MAYBE THERE IS SUCH A THING AS BAD PUBLICITY.

Naturally, there are American black-metal bands as well, including Goatwhore (New Orleans), Leviathan (Chicago), Nachtmystium (Chicago), and Cobalt (Colorado). The American black-metal bands that have caused the greatest stir, however, are Brooklyn's Liturgy and San Francisco's Deafheaven, both of whom have run afoul of tr00 kvltists.

Liturgy's lightning rod is guitarist/vocalist Hunter Hunt-Hendrix, who became infamous for a 2010 manifesto entitled *Transcendental Black Metal: A Vision of Apocalyptic Humanism*. It included such pretentious assertions as this:

> **Transcendental Black Metal is black metal in the mode of Sacrifice. It is a clearing aside of contingent features and a fresh exploration of the essence of black metal. As such it is solar, hypertrophic, courageous, finite and penultimate.**

"The misanthropic aspect of black metal—I couldn't really handle it," Hunt-Hendrix says today. "As I was trying to overcome my teenage college depression, I began to identify a route through European philosophy to start with the misanthropic attitude and then rise out of it, and have a visionary, prophetic, messianic attitude, and pull black metal in that direction, which I think is different than what a lot of people want to do with black metal."

Liturgy quickly became a pariah. "I didn't expect for the metal community to ever find out about Liturgy or the manifesto," Hunt-Hendrix says. "My focus was somewhere else—underground art, music, and philosophy." He has since lost interest in the black metal label. "I'm sure there are new things for the genre to do, but I don't think in those terms any more . . . I don't see any reason for a band to call itself black metal or not."

Deafheaven's alleged transgressions against black metal, meanwhile, are less egregious: its music sounds pretty and its members dress well. Deafheaven's founders, George Clarke (vocals) and Kerry McCoy (guitars), look like normal dudes who might work at a coffee shop; the band's breakthrough album, 2013's *Sunbather*, dared to have a bright pink cover, which was used as part of an Apple keynote presentation announcing the latest model of iPhone.

Alas, as of this writing, tr00 kvltists have yet to find a way to prevent Deafheaven and Liturgy from making music. We wonder why they haven't tried arson yet.

Starter Kit

Ready to become a trOO kvltist?
You will need:

- [ ] ONE (1) SLEEVELESS T-SHIRT, BLACK

- [ ] ONE (1) PAIR JEANS, BLACK

- [ ] ONE (1) PAIR WORK BOOTS, BLACK

- [ ] FACE PAINT, BLACK AND WHITE

- [ ] ONE (1) INVERTED CROSS (PRO TIP: JUST BUY A REGULAR CROSS AND TURN IT UPSIDE DOWN!)

- [ ] *THE SATANIC BIBLE* (1969) BY ANTON SZANDOR LAVEY

- [ ] KEROSENE

- [ ] MATCHES/LIGHTER

- [ ] ONE (1) CONSTITUTION WELL SUITED TO PRISON

- [ ] ONE (1) HATRED OF CHRISTIANITY

Homework

1. **EMPEROR, "I AM THE BLACK WIZARDS"**

   (In the Nightside Eclipse, 1994)

2. **BATHORY, "ENTER THE ETERNAL FIRE"**

   (Under the Sign of the Black Mark, 1987)

3. **MAYHEM, "FREEZING MOON"**

   (De Mysteriis Dom Sathanas, 1994)

4. **DARKTHRONE, "TRANSILVANIAN HUNGER"**

   (Transilvanian Hunger, 1994)

5. **IMMORTAL, "AT THE HEART OF WINTER"**

   (At the Heart of Winter, 1999)

6. **GORGOROTH, "CRUSHING THE SCEPTER (REGAINING A LOST DOMINION)"**

   (Pentagram, 1994)

7. **ENSLAVED, "ISA"**

   (Isa, 2004)

8. **ULVER, "CAPITEL I: I TROLDSKOG FAREN VILD"**

   (Bergtatt—Et eeventyr i 5 capitler, 1995)

9. **SATYRICON, "MOTHER NORTH"**

   (Divina, 1996)

10. **DIMMU BORGIR, "PROGENIES OF THE GREAT APOCALYPSE"**

    (Death Cult Armageddon, 2003)

11. **1349, "I AM ABOMINATION"**

    (Hellfire, 2005)

12. **DARK FUNERAL, "ENRICHED BY EVIL"**

    (Vobiscum Satanas, 1998)

13. **MARDUK, "CHRISTRAPING BLACK METAL"**

    (Panzer Division, 1999)

14. **WATAIN, "SWORN TO THE DARK"**

    (Sworn to the Dark, 2007)

15. **SIGH, "SCARLET DREAM"**

    (Imaginary Sonicscapes, 2001)

16. **CRADLE OF FILTH, "NYMPHETAMINE FIX"**

    (Nymphetamine, 2004)

17. **BEHEMOTH, "HORNS OV BAPHOMET"**

    (Zos Kia Cultus, 2002)

18. **LEVIATHAN, "THE BITTER EMBLEM OF DISSOLVE"**

    (The Tenth Sub Level of Suicide, 2003)

19. **GOATWHORE, "ALCHEMY OF THE BLACK SUN CULT"**

    (A Haunting Curse, 2006)

20. **NACHTMYSTIUM, "GHOSTS OF GRACE"**

    (Assassins: Black Meddle Part 1, 2008)

21. **COBALT, "GIN"**

    (Gin, 2009)

22. **LITURGY, "GENERATION"**

    (Aesthetica, 2011)

23. **DEAFHEAVEN, "DREAM HOUSE"**

    (Sunbather, 2013)

Nergal can't believe it's not butter. Behemoth in Berlin, March 1, 2014.

I ordered that mutton burger RARE, dammit! Turisas at Sonisphere, Knebworth, England, 2010.

A Crash Course in Viking, Pagan, Folk, and Pirate Metal

Viking, pagan, folk, and pirate metal are semi-interchangeable subgenres that offer black metal's celebration of Scandinavian culture without the pesky bigotry and murder. While affecting a look akin to that of Vikings and/or pagans and/or pirates and/or folks, bands in these genres write celebratory-sounding music that draws as heavily from sea shanties and drinking songs as it does from Bolt Thrower and Bathory. They also often embrace the use of instruments that are uncommon in the metal world (e.g., the flute, the accordion, bagpipes, the hurdy-gurdy).

The undisputed kings of Viking metal are Amon Amarth from Tumba, Sweden. Set to galloping rhythms that instill the listener with a sense of adventure and triumph, Amon Amarth's battle anthems are relatively simple and catchier than dried mead. The band's charismatic frontman, Johan Hegg, is 6 feet 6 inches (200 cm), has a salt-and-gold beard that extends to his chest, and rarely performs

Amon Amarth riding a longboat on the River Thames in London, in 2009, like fucking badasses.

with a shirt on, adding to the illusion that the members of Amon Amarth are, indeed, Vikings. (Hegg looks so convincing that he was cast in the 2014 film *Northmen: A Viking Saga*.) The band's live shows include enough windmill-style headbanging to power a small country, and sometimes feature a scale replica of an actual Viking ship.

Finland's Korpiklaani began as a folk-music act before becoming a metal band, and those roots are readily apparent in its fiddle-driven, booze-soaked party songs. Unlike many of its peers, the only danger in which Korpiklaani is interested is the danger of waking up with a hangover.

Korpiklaani was likely an influence on Alestorm, the rare pirate-metal band to hail from outside Scandinavia—specifically, Scotland. As the name suggests, Alestorm

Korpiklaani in New York City, May 4, 2009.

sings about being drunk, being at sea, and being drunk at sea. The band's 2008 debut was called *Captain Morgan's Revenge*, and its mascot looks like a hybrid of the iconic rum emblem and Davy Jones, the octopus-man-pirate from *Pirates of the Caribbean*. Alestorm may also be the world's first polkacore band.

One band that certainly does not have a polka influence is Turisas, also from Finland. The band members perform in *Mad Max*–esque makeshift leather biker armor with crimson-and-black war paint smeared across their faces. Their bombastic music is patently influenced by symphonic power metal, and feels larger than that of many of their peers. Which is not to say they're without a sense of humor: one of the band's biggest hits is a cover of "Rasputin," the 1978 disco song by Germany's Boney M.

Týr, from the Faroe Islands, also has a clear power-metal influence, but its sound is considerably stripped-down. Týr's riffs, rhythms, lyrical subject matter, and use of sea shanty–esque choruses sung by large groups of men distinctly mark it as a Viking/pagan-metal band. But it's never had a keyboard player, let alone an accordion player. Besides Amon Amarth, Týr is probably as close to more traditional forms of metal as bands in this genre get.

On the poppier side of the spectrum is Eluveitie. The band is from Zurich, Switzerland, but its songs sound distinctly Celtic and often utilize instruments from that culture (e.g., the gaita, the bodhrá, and the Celtic harp). There's something about this element of the band's music that gives it a distinctly romantic quality, which is bolstered by the frequent use of Evanescence-esque female vocals in addition to the more traditional growls provided by frontman and multi-instrumentalist Chrigel Glanzmann.

Those seeking something a little proggier should look to Helsinki, the city that spawned both Moonsorrow and Wintersun. Despite their monikers referencing celestial beings, the two bands actually don't have very much in common. Wintersun, founded by former Ensiferum member Jari Mäenpää, is

basically a proggy melodeath band with synths that are as likely to sound like accordions as they are to sound like a choir of singing glasses. Moonsorrow, meanwhile, has accurately classified its music as "epic heathen metal." The band writes ambitious, sprawling, atmospheric sagas that seamlessly incorporate a wide variety of metallic subgenres. Its albums don't contain songs so much as they contain movements. That's not just a critic's flowery praise: most of their best material is at least ten minutes long. Moonsorrow's live shows are equally enchanting experiences, as likely to inspire stunned awe as they are mosh pits.

There is also a band called Finntroll. You know everything there is to know about it from the fact that its members call themselves "Finntroll."

Extra Credit

1. AMON AMARTH, "THE PURSUIT OF VIKINGS"
(Fate of Norns, 2004)

2. KORPIKLAANI, "WOODEN PINTS"
(Spirit of the Forest, 2003)

3. TURISAS, "STAND UP AND FIGHT"
(Stand Up and Fight, 2012)

4. ELUVEITIE, "THE CALL OF THE MOUNTAINS"
(Origins, 2014)

5. MOONSORROW, "PIMEÄ"
(Verisäkeet, 2005)

Well, **FUCK** you and **FUCK** this 7-Eleven parking lot! Pantera in Chicago, Illinois, in 1992.

A Crash Course in Groove Metal and Sludge

Groove metal and sludge occur when you take all the high parts out of metal—the twiddling solos, the shrieked vocals, the rat-a-tat cymbals. The result sounds soulful rather than cheesy, which appealed to the glam-exhausted fans of the early '90s, who loved to smoke weed but still weren't sold on the cynicism of grunge, the whininess of alternative, or the fishnets of goth and industrial.

Perhaps the fist true groove metal bands were New Orleans's Exhorder, whose fuzzy guitar tone was uniquely sexy; and New York City's Prong, whose weirdo conceptual thrash went more for kinetic impact than grandiosity. However, groove metal's real claims to fame are two of metal's most important bands regardless of genre.

Texas's Pantera started as a typical glam-metal band, a fact that will forever be pointed out by metalheads who want to laugh at tough guys in spandex. However, Pantera had real chops in the form of guitarist "Diamond" Darrell Abbot, a hard-drinking guitar god with a heart of gold. When the band gained wily, Venom-obsessed singer Phil Anselmo, it adopted a troubled dirt-bag persona that added a grinding harshness to its sound. "Diamond" Darrell became "Dimebag" Darrell, and Pantera released five near-perfect albums that drew a new generation of fans to heavy music. The band's 1992 album *Vulgar Display of Power*

features a dude getting punched in the face on its cover, and it sounds like it looks.

Sadly, Pantera's legacy is forever mired in misery and controversy. After the release of 2000's *Reinventing the Steel*, the band broke up, and during a 2004 performance with his post-Pantera band Damageplan, Darrell was shot and killed by a mentally unstable fan. The fallout from his death was monumental—Pantera drummer and Darrell's brother Vinnie Paul blamed Phil, Phil lashed out at Vinnie Paul, and everyone was heartbroken. Anselmo also became known for going on racially charged rants onstage; as of 2016, he's still at it, having

White Zombie versus a smoke machine in Minneapolis, Minnesota, May 13, 1995.

WHITE ZOMBIE

MAKE THEM DIE SLOWLY

album contained "More Human Than Human," a shrieking sex anthem found on the soundtrack of every '90s action movie.

Rob Zombie left the band in 1998 and began a lucrative solo career with the 1998 monster-rock epic *Hellbilly Deluxe*. He has since become a successful horror director, making 2003's slasher opus *House of a Thousand Corpses* and 2007's lackluster remake of John Carpenter's *Halloween*. Yseult has played in other bands, none as good as White Zombie.

As groove metal became the mainstream, its drug-addled cousin, sludge, pervaded the underground. Sludge sounds like groove metal on heroin, its raw disillusionment attracting blue-collar lowlifes who could relate to both the music's hypnotic riffs and its themes of American decay.

The biggest sludge bands are Crowbar and Eyehategod, both of whom hail from New Orleans and featured drummer Jimmy Bower. Crowbar is fronted by Kirk "Riff Lord" Windstein and draws more from hardcore than anything else; its music sounds like the first three seconds after getting hit extremely hard in the jaw. Eyehategod, meanwhile, is just ugly as fuck. The band's lead singer, Mike Williams, sounds like he's trying to get the last of the sick out, and its song subjects range from drug use ("Take as Needed for Pain") to feeling really fucking bad about yourself ("Robitussin and Rejection"). In many ways, Eyehategod is America's answer to black metal—it's couched

screamed "WHITE POWER!" at the audience at a show in honor of Dimebag's legacy.

White Zombie was a hybrid of American coastal music scenes—New York City's artsy grime and L.A.'s chill weirdness. The band started with art-school dropouts Rob Zombie (né Straker, né Cummings), on vocals, and Sean Yseult, on bass, making mind-bending noise rock with grindhouse horror themes. Bit by bit, the band's sound hardened into blood-hungry garage metal, resulting in two monumental albums, 1992's *La Sexercisto: Devil Music Vol. I* and 1995's semi-industrial *Astro-Creep: 2000 Songs of Love, Destruction, and Other Synthetic Delusions of the Electric Head*. The former took off when its first single, "Thunderkiss '65," was featured on MTV's *Beavis and Butt-Head* and received glowing praise from the imbeciles thereon. The latter

Eyehategod: this is as close to smiling as you're going to get.

in the classic traditions of its homeland, but focuses entirely on the most twisted parts of them.

These days, groove metal and sludge have evolved—the former is what every classic thrash band plays since its comeback (Destruction, Kreator, Death Angel), while the latter has found mainstream recognition with the growing popularity of doom metal (Mastodon, Neurosis, Celtic Frost's last album). For one brief moment, though, these genres were the truest metal in town, and headbangers still cling to them for fear that the post-grunge slump of the '90s might happen again.

Extra Credit

1. PRONG, "SNAP YOUR FINGERS, SNAP YOUR NECK"
(Cleansing, 1994)

2. PANTERA, "WALK"
(Vulgar Display of Power, 1992)

3. WHITE ZOMBIE, "THUNDERKISS '65"
(La Sexorcisto: Devil Music Vol. 1, 1992)

4. EYEHATEGOD, "SISTER FUCKER (PT. 1)"
(Take as Needed For Pain)

5. CROWBAR, "PLANETS COLLIDE"
(Odd Fellows Rest, 2002)

Doom Metal

WHAT IS IT?

Weed-fueled stoner rock tinged with an arch hatred for mankind.

WHO LISTENS TO IT?

Nerdy potheads in patch-covered denim who worship Satan by smelling like a goat and getting super fucked up.

WHERE DOES IT COME FROM?

The Pacific Northwest, Arkansas, Colorado . . . and also Sweden, for some weird reason.

BASTARD CHILDREN:

Funeral doom, suicidal doom, experimental doom, stoner doom, blackened doom, sludge.

THE BIG FOUR:

Trouble, Saint Vitus, Candlemass, High on Fire.

Jesus, what happened to Rush?! Pentagram at the Gramercy Theatre in New York, 2014.

 he earliest known use of marijuana for its physical effects occurred in 2727 B.C., when the Chinese Emperor Shen Nung used cannabis to ease his rheumatism. Since then (and likely before), Satan's broccoli has been a sacrament and medicine for the blues of being alive. Hindus in ancient India and Nepal used it for religious purposes, calling it ganja. Rock music obtained it through bluesmen who smoked it as a cheap tobacco alternative. It became a sensation when Bob Dylan introduced it to the Beatles. Its influence on music after that is widely known, a third-eye-opening experience that ushered in an era of harmony and love.

By the time Black Sabbath wrote their marijuana anthem "Sweet Leaf," however, love had failed, and only the weed remained. These guys weren't going to give up the thing that blew their minds just because everything else sucked; if anything, weed was needed to alleviate the

TROUBLE

PSALM 9

bummer's ill effects. Marijuana is treated like a new friend in "Sweet Leaf" rather than a cosmic force—Sabbath had already seen the light; they just needed something to give them a hand.

Bands with a similar romantic potheadedness carried Black Sabbath's torch, making loud sorcerer's blues. In that way, doom metal will forever be pure, because it stems directly from Sabbath. It's metal that went into the family business.

One of weed's most notable influences on doom metal is that doom is pretty listenable. Even the catchiest black or death metal band requires some musical fortitude to stomach, but doom-metal songs normally have a 4/4 rhythm and a verse/chorus setup that appeals to the average listener.

Who doesn't love Christian metal? Trouble in Chicago, March 1990.

Wino kills a poser with his fucking mind at the With Full Force Festival in Germany, 2003.

Some vocalists still scream and shriek, but bands like Burning Witch and Weedeater sound more primal than they do evil. Simply put, the relentless blast-beats and frenetic rhythms of extreme metal can be difficult to headbang to, but there is nothing easier than headbanging to a doom song.

One of the earliest bands that could be called "doom metal" proper was Pentagram, from Virginia. Guitarist Geof O'Keefe and bug-eyed singer Bobby Liebling formed the band in homage to the heavy proto-metal bands like Sabbath and UFO and played 'lude'd-out van rock with a hard satanic vibe, thus cementing a place of image in underground metal. With his scarecrow-thin body, Brillo Pad hair, and terrifying thousand-yard stare, Liebling looks like a giant spider wearing

the decomposing corpse of a high school theater kid. But the voice coming out of his wiry frame is powerful, full of convincing drama and evil soul. Liebling's substance abuse was also very real—a documentary titled *Last Days Here* about Liebling's career and struggles with addiction was released in 2011, and helped return the band to national and international attention.

But the genre had to escape the boundaries of mere Iommi copycatting, and it did so with Trouble from Aurora, Illinois. Arriving on the scene a few years after Pentagram, Trouble brought a heavier riff, a high shrieked vocal, and a more dynamic sense of madness to doom. The result was cryptic biker rock laced with self-doubt and outlaw philosophy, providing a respite from every other

Saint Vitus looking exactly as you imagine them, circa 2003.

band attempting to sound like heroin wizards. In fact, vocalist Eric Wagner openly wrote anti-satanic lyrics, leading the band's label, Metal Blade, to sell them as "white metal," in opposition to the black-metal sound espoused by Venom, Mercyful Fate, and Celtic Frost.

Similar to Trouble was Los Angeles–based doom crew Saint Vitus, who wrote gloomy, scrappy heavy-rock songs about shadows, crypts, and not giving a fuck. Saint Vitus's guitar tone went impressively far on the fuzzy end of the spectrum, while the echoing space behind drummer Armando Acosta's percussion made it sound as though every song were performed in an ancient castle. The band was pointedly misanthropic, enjoying outsider status in an era when a poppy hook was king. The chorus of the band's 1987 ode to metalheaddom, "Born Too Late," ends with Wino screaming, "And I'll never be like you."

Though Saint Vitus had several lineup changes throughout its career, the band will forever be known for the albums it recorded with vocalist Scott Weinrich, better known as "Wino." Famous for fronting both Vitus and the highly popular stoner-rock powerhouse the Obsessed, Wino is the embodiment of doom metal as its own genre and he has risen to Lemmy-esque levels of regard in the underground for his consistent ability to walk the walk. Because of doom's appreciation for, or at least sympathy with, outsiders and outlaws, it would be nearly impossible for Wino to cause a scandal; when he was deported from Norway mid-tour for possession of methamphetamine in 2014, the public response seemed to be a shrug. (Wino, it should be noted, publicly apologized to fans and his bandmates for the incident.)

"I was always drawn to the sadder stuff," says Wino. "The more minor than major stuff. There's just something inside me personally—the type of music that moved my spirit or my soul was the darker stuff. It might come from past lives. We've been conditioned not to remember the thousands of years our spirits lived. But it's also a gut thing. I'll take Joy Division over any number of modern so-called 'doom bands.' People trying to be a doom band, that's trying a little bit too hard."

One thing that sets Vitus apart from many other bands is that its purpose is positive. Just like Black Sabbath before them, Saint Vitus's music preaches hope—if only for the dirt-bags and weirdoes. Though songs like "Born Too Late" or the apocalyptic anthem "The Waste of Time" seem to describe a state of conflict, it is born out of tension with an unfair and backward world.

"It's hard to wrap your head around the bad shit," says Wino. "The music should be, and my music has always been, about finding the silver lining. Why else would you want to get out of bed every day and pick up the guitar?"

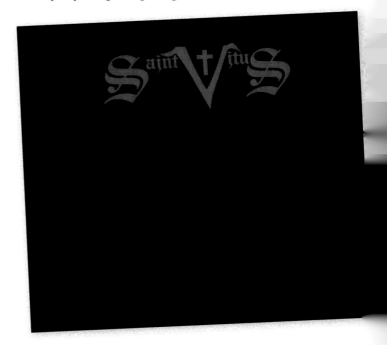

INSERT SCREW 1 INTO SLOT A! Candlemass, circa 1988.

APPARENTLY, PEOPLE SMOKE POT IN SWEDEN

The name "doom metal" makes sense. With its groaning minor chord guitars and steady, zombie-shuffle rhythms, doom channels a cinematic atmosphere of dread that connects with the mind of the ferociously stoned. If thrash is the atom bomb, black metal the hand that pushes the button, and death metal the shockwave blast ripping meat from the skeletons of schoolchildren, then doom metal is the nuclear winter, the darkening skies and the creeping terror that comes with them.

In a piece for *Bandcamp Daily* titled "Doom Metal: A Brief Timeline," journalist Jon Wiederhorn describes the genre's eternal message:

Doom affects the gut and the psyche, conveying sensations of darkness and foreboding with fuzzed out guitars, mid-paced tempos and generally morose vocals. Groove is paramount, as is a certain amount of repetition, generally achieved with crunching, palm-muted guitar chords, complementary, minor key melodies and rhythms that wax and wane, only to rise again . . . But even without the musical modifications, doom is forever because dread and grief are universal—and musicians will always be drawn to express universal feelings of anger, hopelessness, fear, and sadness.

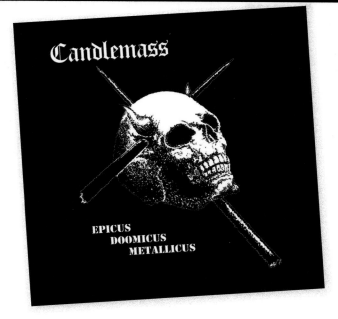

"I never really thought of the Obsessed as a doom band," says Wino. "I guess Vitus were pretty doom-y, but I always thought of us more as stoner rock. The first time I heard 'doom metal' was probably when Candlemass used it."

In 1986, Swedish doom band Candlemass released its debut album, *Epicus Doomicus Metallicus*, which not only gave doom its name but also redefined the genre with the addition of double-bass drums and frontman Johan Längqvist's dramatic intonations.

Perhaps it was the fact that Candlemass hailed from Europe, where weed was seen as more of an eye-opener than a cause of teenage pregnancies, but the band's doom had a greater sense of scope than that of its peers. Where other doom bands sounded like they were entirely raised on Sabbath and '70s death rock, Candlemass was weaned on Iron Maiden and Mercyful Fate, its lyrics full of mossy stone crypts and haggard necromancers. For some, this was cheesy as hell, a level of oblivious seriousness applied to a genre birthed in the dank crucible of a bong hit. But for many everyday

metalheads who were more interested in high-flying escapism than smoking a roach while living in a squat, it made doom metal accessible.

Not only accessible, but not, well, boring. Sure, Pentagram and Saint Vitus's crawling pace appealed to cloudy-minded headbangers, but their songs often took forever and rarely changed up the pace. Even Sabbath played fast sometimes. Candlemass's riffs had Judas Priest-ian momentum, and though tracks like "Mirror Mirror" and "At the Gallows' End" were slower than Metallica, they still felt like they were going somewhere. This paved the way for burgeoning doom bands like British powerhouse Cathedral and New Orleans sludge-rockers Crowbar to use hard-hitting riffs to keep their music entertaining.

Behind the scenes, Candlemass was a bit of a mess. The band could never hold down a lineup, with a revolving door of members, save for founding bassist Leif Edling. Despite its unstable roster, Candlemass consistently released powerful metal—so much so that in 2013, *Sweden Rock Magazine* named Candlemass the greatest Swedish metal band of all time.[1]

I   Which, for the record, is a big deal in Sweden.

EVERYONE KNOWS YOU'RE HIGH

Trouble and Saint Vitus also freed doom metal from the shackles of Satan. When '80s metal became obsessed with Devil worship, doom metal took a step back. Glam's demonology was sleazy and reactionary, and thrash's was profoundly angry; doom didn't want anything to do with either. The genre appreciated the spooky atmosphere of '70s horror films, but a human mind fractured by mushrooms was hell enough.

Accordingly, doom metal carved out its own personality and style. Its fans were often thoughtful, refreshingly old-school, sometimes smelly, and always wasted. Their adherence to tradition and acceptance of political theory made them friendly with the crust-punk scene, which appreciated doom's lack of hygienic emphasis and its use of riffs even polluted people could bounce along to.

By the '90s, as traditional metal began fading into the underground, doom metal stopped being a tribute genre, and its influence was felt throughout many of rock's subcultures. The Melvins (see A Crash Course in Alternative Metal, page 117) utilized doom's patented punch and stony self-awareness, while Type O Negative (see A Crash Course in Goth Metal, page 145) merged doom's brooding atmosphere with goth's stylized shadow to create music that sounded like an eyeliner-smeared orgy. In Nashville, Tennessee, Today Is the Day was making a disturbing racket, while in

Electric Wizard before they knew they were Electric Wizard, at Obsessions in Randolph, New Jersey, in 1991.

Maryland a band called Clutch merged garage-y doom and DC boogie music, with fascinating and fun results. After periods of obsession with thrash's speed, death metal's horror, black metal's darkness, and nu metal's vulgarity, the metal scene finally began maturing into doom.

"I think one of the reasons this happened is because doom is in some ways an old man's game," says Ben Hutcherson, guitarist and vocalist for Denver doom-metal band Khemmis. Khemmis's sophomore album, *Hunted*, is a doom-metal masterpiece and was voted *Decibel* magazine's 2016 "Album of the Year." "The older you get, the more appealing less complicated things are. Emotive bands start to resonate. When I was younger, I thought of doom as the music that old stoners play, and now that I'm older, I play it all the time."

Few bands paved the way for doom's evolution more than Oakland's Neurosis, which seemed uninterested in expressing anguish via stereotypical means, opting instead for discordant riffs and howled psychedelic lyrics. The band, led

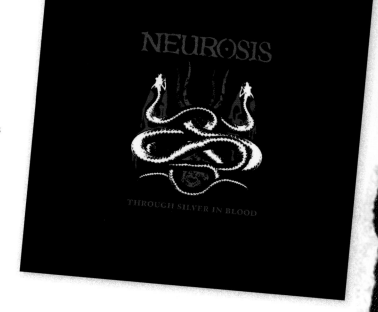

by visionary vocalist and guitarist Scott Kelly, mixed metal and hardcore and then stretched it out over sprawling periods of time, creating primal, heavy rock straight from the womb. While certain Neurosis albums thrive on harsh punchiness, it is the black hole singularity of 1996's *Through Silver in Blood* that made Neurosis a dysfunctional household name.

Of the Sabbath clones, the best was British stoners Electric Wizard. In the church of weed, Electric Wizard is the undisputed high priest, its fuzz-drenched riffs like the onset of good Indica-dominant bud you got from your roommate's boyfriend. The band's lyrics focus on smoking weed ("Incense for the Damned"), classic horror ("We Live"), or monsters from classic horror smoking weed ("The Satanic Rites of Drugula"). The cover of the band's breakthrough album, 2000's *Dopethrone*, portrays the great god Pan taking a bong rip. Other doom bands, such as Wisconsin's punishing Bongzilla and North Carolina's scathing Weedeater (who might win the award for Best Album Title Parody with 2001's *. . . And Justice for Y'All*), courted a similarly blatant relationship with the Devil's lettuce.

DOOM METAL

187

Sleep forgetting where they are: the Limelight, New York City, February 1993.

THE PATRON SAINT OF THE SHIRTLESS

While Electric Wizard always remained underground in its hyper-satanic drug lust, another band made being openly baked a state that everyone could admit to.

Matt Pike got involved in doom metal in the early 1990s when he left military school in Colorado and arrived in California. He joined the band Asbestosdeath, which was then playing mostly stripped-down sludge. Eventually, its sound took a Sabbathian turn toward thickset stoner rock. In an attempt, one assumes, to attract fans to its slowly growing following, the band changed its name to Sleep—an ominous moniker in its own right.

Sleep sounds sweaty. Pike's throbbing, abrasive guitar tone doesn't mimic the wild celebration of Jimi Hendrix, but rather the steely assault of Trouble. The band appealed not only to metalheads who were doing their best to abandon hair metal in search of true heaviness but also to the hardcore

kids who liked loud-ass music with a steady rhythm that felt to some extent like being struck physically.

Delightfully, the band's success meant that when its members decided to leave Earache Records due to poor interactions with the famously toxic label head Digby Pearson, they were snapped up by major label London Records. Sadly, this put a lot of pressure on them to deliver palatable material—which, as any introspective stoner can tell you, does not always work out. The band's final album, which features an hour-long song named "Dopesmoker," perplexed the employees at London; though recorded in 1996, *Dopesmoker* wasn't released until 2003, on Southern Lord Records.

Frustrated with having its creativity compromised, Sleep split up in 1998. That same year, Pike began jamming with friends in Sleep's practice space and put together a winning combination—him on guitar and vocals, Des Kensel on drums, and George Rice on bass. Casting subtlety and mainstream acceptance to the wind, he made his favorite pastime pretty blatant with the name of his new band: High on Fire.

Almost from the moment of formation, High on Fire became the coolest band on the planet. The slow, pounding heaviness of Sleep was still there— Pike's guitar tone sounds similar in both bands— but the speed and aggression of the music increased tenfold, adding a sharp edge and a dynamic dance to Pike's riffs. By giving doom speed and heaviness, High on Fire reinvigorated the genre, making it possible to appreciate while throwing elbows in a mosh pit. For modern metal fans who'd grown up on both the Melvins and Motörhead, the band's sound was a liberating indulgence in everything they loved. Its music is as much about the fan with the black-light poster as the epic scene the poster

depicts. Its concerts are feral bacchanals. Pike's vicious riffs and compulsive shirtlessness made him the sweaty, brilliant poster boy of modern doom metal.

High on Fire has released seven full-length studio albums to date, and each one is better than the last. The band's legacy lives on, not only in its history, but also in that of other bands. At a 2000 High on Fire show in Atlanta, four dudes met and decided to jam together; the band they formed, Mastodon, would go on to dominate the world with

Oh, hell and damn yes. High on Fire at New England Metal and Hardcore Festival, Worcester, Massachusetts, 2008.

high on fire

blessed black wings

music very much like that of High on Fire (see Metalcore, page 233).

Matt Pike got sober in 2012, after confessing that he was killing himself slowly with booze. Some feared that his unhinged talent might be dulled by giving up liquor, but in 2015 the band released *Luminiferous*, its tightest, most violent record to date, reassuring fans and shutting up naysayers once and for all. It helps, of course, that Pike still smokes weed.

BUZZ: HARSHED

As metal entered a new millennium, doom metal came back into the spotlight hard. This happened for a lot of reasons, including that doom existed as the complete antithesis of nu metal, the most popular metallic subgenre of the late '90s and early 2000s. Nu metal was kinetic, catchy, speedy, and immature, thriving on sonic novelty and embracing the terror of a digital age. But doom sounded old when it was created, and tapped into those things that metalheads growing up in the age of Linkin Park felt nostalgic for: big riffs, weird tales, denim, leather, and good old-fashioned weed.

One musician who seemed especially attuned to doom's return was Nirvana drummer and Foo Fighters frontman Dave Grohl. In 2004, Grohl released the self-titled debut album by his band Probot, a passion project that saw him playing all the instruments with a rotating cast of classic metal frontmen. While Grohl's rogue's gallery featured the usual suspects—King Diamond, Lemmy, Max Cavalera—the album also included tracks sung by the likes Trouble's Eric Church, Cathedral's Lee Dorrian, and Wino.

As doom began to mature, new bands with unique sounds emerged. The hipster scene in Oregon, known for creating artsy black-metallers Agalloch, also spawned Yob, whose endless, gigantic riffs inspired a legion of headbangers to go for a walk in the woods. The humidity-choked swamps of New Orleans coughed up sludge (see A Crash Course in Groove Metal and Sludge, page 172), a form of doom metal with heavy doses of hardcore; the subgenre's most important band, Eyehategod, sounded heavy and smoked weed, but also did every other drug on the planet and sang about incest.

The dream team: Dave Grohl, Lemmy, and Wino together as Probot, Los Angeles, California, November 2003.

"Bands like Eyehategod, that are as influenced by Sabbath as they are Black Flag, really appealed to extreme metal fans," says Hutcherson. "A lot of older heads in the scene that play in established doom bands started off as punk rock kids. Mike Scheidt [of Yob], who is now the spiritual guru of the doom metal scene, talks a lot about growing up a punk-rock kid. I think there's a set of emotions that exist in hardcore that crosses over well into doom. It's not a huge change, to slow things down."

Little Rock, Arkansas, also produced two of the most important and listenable doom bands of all time. Rwake are huge, dynamic, and actively ugly, sounding like a cut of *Requiem for a Dream* where the moon collides with the earth midway through. The band's frontman, Christopher Farris Terry—C. T. to anyone who's ever met him—became widely known for a) being a stand-up dude who fights for metal's right to rock, and b) drinking tons of cough syrup while playing live. (The band's name is pronounced "wake," with the *R* inserted as a reference to Robitussin.) In an interview with *Revolver* in 2011, C. T. didn't beat around the issue:

I mean, we don't only drink cough syrup, and we don't do it as much as we used to, but we're really down with the totally awesome way it feels. It's crazy how some fans take it to heart—we have kids in the front row of our shows where I'm like, "Dude, you're a fucking zombie." It's just our thing. Especially in small town spaces—a lot of kids around here will chug cough syrup, or huff shit, whatever's over the counter. That's where we come from, that's who we are.

Little Rock also produced Pallbearer, one of doom's most undeniably impressive young talents. Pallbearer's music is compelling and fuzzy, but it utilizes echoing melancholy to make it emotionally resonant. Its albums consistently rule, but no two records sound quite the same.

"While New Orleans's sound was based on anger, the Arkansas sound was based on despondency," adds Hutcherson. "It's really easy to feel lost living in the south if you're into anything deviant, like having long hair. A lot of that feeling adrift informs why Arkansas is able to make the bands it does. That comes across with Pallbearer's stuff—they sound more triumphant than Rwake, but they still have a particular kind of sadness to their melodies and sonic aesthetic . . . there's something cultural and geographic about it."

Doom also began infiltrating other genres of metal, especially death metal, which appreciated the ominousness of doom's riffs and its obsession with 1970s horror (death metal bands like Autopsy and Asphyx had been slowing things down for a while already, so the transition felt natural). Finland's Hooded Menace creates oozing doom-death, their name a reference to the Spanish cult horror film *Tombs of the Blind Dead* (1972). Detroit's Acid Witch gurgles about pot-smoking swamp sorceresses over keyboard-highlighted riffs. Japan's two death/doom bands, Coffins and Church of Misery, slowed down death metal's chug with absolutely punishing results. Black metal stars also got in on the game: Triptykon, the latest band by Hellhammer and Celtic Frost frontman Tom G. Warrior, contains as much doom as it does black metal, using the former's weight and tempo to enhance the latter's sense of shadow and darkness.

As doom metal continues to expand its horizons, more and more mainstream listeners enjoy its closeness to Black Sabbath's early sound and its celebration of smoking weed. It's only a matter of time before the stars of the genre are approached by those of hip-hop for collaboration, as both schools of music possess hipster cred, appreciation for old-school traditions, and a love of getting high as hell.

Starter Kit

Dude, are you cool? Do you party? Then you'll need:

☐ 1 OZ. SCHWAG WEED WITH HAIRS AND SHIT IN IT

☐ 3.2 GRAMS GOOD BANANA KUSH FOR YOUR FRIENDS

☐ 0.2 GRAMS COKE FROM THE OTHER NIGHT

☐ THREE (3) LOOSE ROLLING PAPERS IN YOUR POCKET

☐ ONE (1) PAIR SKINNY JEANS, RIPPED

☐ ONE (1) DENIM JACKET, ALSO RIPPED

☐ 1.6 FT. HAIR, UNWASHED

☐ ONE (1) OUTDATED CAR WORTH $2,500 OR LESS

☐ FIVE (5) CASSETTES, ONE OF WHICH IS NEUROSIS'S *THROUGH SILVER IN BLOOD*

☐ A PASSING CURIOSITY AS TO WHERE YOU ARE AND HOW YOU GOT THERE

Homework

1. BLACK SABBATH, "SWEET LEAF"
(Masters of Reality, 1971)

2. TROUBLE, "VICTIM OF THE INSANE"
(Psalm 9, 1984)

3. PENTAGRAM, "THE GHOUL"
(Relentless, 1985)

4. SAINT VITUS, "WHITE MAGIC/ BLACK MAGIC"
(Saint Vitus, 1984)

5. CANDLEMASS, "SOLITUDE"
(Epicus Doomicus Metallicus, 1986)

6. SLEEP, "THE DRUID"
(Sleep's Holy Mountain, 1993)

7. TROUBLE, "THE WOLF"
(Trouble, 1990)

8. SAINT VITUS, "BORN TOO LATE"
(Born Too Late, 1986)

9. PENTAGRAM, "EVIL SEED"
(Day of Reckoning, 1987)

10. CATHEDRAL, "FANGALACTICUS SUPERGORIA"
(The Carnival Bizarre, 1995)

11. KYUSS, "DEMON CLEANER"
(Welcome to Sky Valley, 1994)

12. NEUROSIS, "THROUGH SILVER IN BLOOD"
(Through Silver in Blood, 1996)

13. HIGH ON FIRE, "BLESSED BLACK WINGS"
(Blessed Black Wings, 2005)

14. RWAKE, "DYING SPIRAL GALAXIES"
(If You Walk Before You Crawl, You Crawl Before You Die, 2004)

15. ELECTRIC WIZARD, "EKO EKO AZARAK: INVOCATION/RITUAL"
(We Live, 2004)

16. PROBOT, "THE EMERALD LAW" (FEAT. WINO)
(Probot, 2004)

17. BURNING WITCH, "COUNTRY DOCTOR"
(Crippled Lucifer, 2009)

18. KYLESA, "DROP OUT"
(Spiral Shadow, 2010)

19. HIGH ON FIRE, "KING OF DAYS"
(De Vermis Mysteriis, 2012)

20. HOODED MENACE, "CHASM OF THE WRAITH"
(Labyrinth of Carrion Breeze EP, 2014)

21. PALLBEARER, "THORNS"
(The Thorns single, 2017

22. KHEMMIS, "CANDLELIGHT"
(Hunted, 2016)

23. CLUTCH, "THE FACE"
(Earth Rocker, 2013)

Zakk Wylde romancing the female chaperones at Ozzfest 2001, in California.

Metal Festivals: Massive Aggressive

The experience of seeing metal played live is a great way to a) find out which bands are really talented and which ones rely on studio magic, and b) meet other metalheads in your area with whom you share musical taste and establish what's commonly referred to as a "scene." In these ways, metal is made for festivals—multi-day gauntlets of classic bands and bright new talent that draw in fans from all over the world to mingle with one another and trade vinyl.

Metal fests are not for the weak of heart. Make no mistake, if you want to get a day ticket and catch a bunch of bands surrounded by people, that's easy enough. But it takes a champion to survive three to four days of nonstop live drums, shameless day-drinking, smelly outdoor camping, and interacting with thousands of people as misanthropic as they are sweaty. If you think you're up to the task, here are the major meccas worth hitting:

MEDIA

Wacken survival tip: drink all the beer before anyone else can.

WACKEN OPEN AIR

Located in a cow pasture some forty-five miles north of Hamburg, Germany, Wacken is the largest metal-only festival in the world. It draws about eighty thousand headbangers from around the globe, creating a heavy-metal shantytown for the last weekend of August. Every fan should go to Wacken once—seeing your favorite obscure black-metal band playing a huge stage to thousands of chanting fans is a mind-blowing experience—but they should bring baby wipes and blister cream.

DOWNLOAD FESTIVAL

Download takes place at Donington Park in Leicestershire, England, and is the modern successor of the Monsters of Rock Festival that was a mainstay of metal culture in the 1980s (the phrase "Donington" is often used to lump both festivals together). Unlike Monsters,

Download showcases a wide variety of rock with distortion, with everyone from ska-punks Reel Big Fish to slam brutes Dying Fetus having played the fest. In 2009, the festival had an estimated 120,000 attendees over three days.

OZZFEST

Ozzfest was the ultimate Americanization of the metal festival—a traveling, single-day event featuring only the most popular bands in aggressive rock. But American audiences

Black Sabbath owning Ozzfest (literally), Los Angeles, September 24, 2016.

it, and Ozzy and Sharon's traveling soon went international and became the nt of every suburban metalhead's year. ur launched the careers of many popular tal bands like Slipknot and metalcore like Killswitch Engage. Ozzfest continues out in a much diminished capacity, and and 2017 required Slipknot's single-day ng Knotfest to even prop it up.

R NOTABLE FESTS

LAND DEATHFEST: An annual extreme-estival in Baltimore that features the the underground. Gross, drunken, and tely worth attending at least once.

POP METAL MEETING: A massive metal l in Dessel, Belgium, that features big cal acts like Rammstein, Black Sabbath, pknot. Consistently one of the best s in the metal festival calendar.

FEST: The biggest French metal festival, for featuring both gigantic-name hard nd metal acts and packing in a solid

number of underground legends every year. Has tenuous relations with the French government, which tried to shut it down in 2016 when the fest refused to drop Down, the side project of Pantera frontman Phil Anselmo, who'd just been accused of racism.

70,000 TONS OF METAL: The biggest and oldest of the metal cruises—as in, a metal festival on a cruise ship, buffet and all. Small by fest standards—only about four thousand attendees—but the cruise aspect takes the madness to a different level. Hellishly expensive, but a lot of fun.

PSYCHO LAS VEGAS: A stoner, doom, biker, and classic rock festival in Sin City. Also features weirdo acts like Wolves in the Throne Room and Khemmis. Thankfully, it's Vegas, so there are drugs everywhere.

THE GATHERING OF THE JUGGALOS: The Insane Clown Posse's annual festival. Features some surprisingly strong metal, like Cannibal Corpse and Soulfly. Really just about hooking up with a fat person while drinking cheap soda pop.

METAL FESTIVALS: MASSIVE AGGRESSIVE

Trent Reznor of Nine Inch Nails, possibly fighting to hold back a massive dump.

A Crash Course in Industrial

Industrial is a subgenre that crossbreeds metal with electronic music. Like glam and nu metal, industrial is much maligned by metal purists. This is partially due to the fact that industrial's reliance on computer technology is viewed as an undermining of legitimate musicianship, partially because metal purists are close-minded schmucks, and partially because industrial tends to be mopey and goth'd out.

England's Killing Joke, which basically sounds like a slightly more upbeat version of the Cure, was one of the first rock bands to incorporate elements of electronica into its work, and is thus generally considered proto-industrial. The genre's true originators include Chicago's Ministry, Germany's KMFDM, and England's Godflesh. KMFDM leans closest to the EDM side of the spectrum. Metal dudes are apt to give Ministry props because frontman Al Jourgensen has a ton of piercings, a "fuck you" attitude, and a history of hanging out with people way cooler than him, such as Timothy Leary and William S. Burroughs, but its songs tend to be so long and repetitive that it's difficult to imagine anyone actually enjoying them without the aid of potent psychedelics. Godflesh is the most undeniably metal of the three groups. The duo includes Justin Broadrick, who also co-founded Napalm Death, and its music tends to be pretty heavy.

Godflesh certainly inspired Los Angeles's Fear Factory, whose earliest recordings sounded as though Broadrick himself had written them. The band's vocalist, Burton C. Bell, also loves to write cyberpunk-esque lyrics about the Singularity and whatnot. But Fear Factory found greater success catering to the death- and nu-metal crowds rather than industrial fans. This is largely due to the fact that the band's guitarist, Dino Cazares, has death-metal cred, having also co-founded the deathgrind band Brujeria.

Godflesh's influence is also clear in the music of Nailbomb, a project created by Sepultura's Max Cavalera and Fudge Tunnel's Alex Newport. The band only ever made one studio album, 1994's *Point Blank*, but it remains a favorite of people who were in the prime of their youth when it was released.

KMFDM's native Germany also produced one of industrial's most commercially successful acts, Rammstein. The band's songs are simple, catchy, and cinematic, and its

Godflesh performing in New Jersey, November 1996.

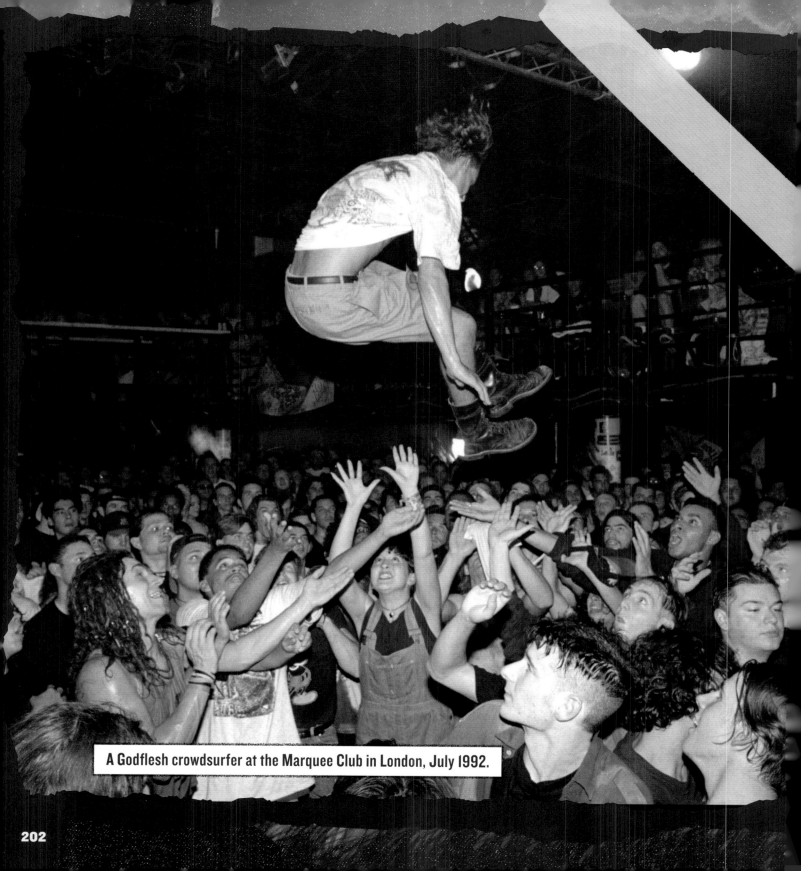

A Godflesh crowdsurfer at the Marquee Club in London, July 1992.

sold-out arena performances include fire and lasers galore, as well as a healthy dose of homoeroticism.

Industrial's brightest star, however, is Trent Reznor, who writes, records, and tours with a rotating cast of musicians under the name Nine Inch Nails. Reznor applied pop structure to industrial metal, which kicked open the door to the MTV audience that eluded bands like Godflesh. What's more, Reznor's distinctly emo vibe was a perfect fit for the Cobain generation of Debbie Downers. Nine Inch Nails continues to be a mega-success to this day, and in 2011, Reznor and his frequent collaborator, Atticus Ross, won an Oscar for their work on David Fincher's *The Social Network*.

In 1992, Reznor launched his own label, Nothing Records. His first signing, Marilyn Manson, was also his most successful. Manson initially achieved notoriety in 1994, thanks to his creepy cover of Eurythmics' "Sweet Dreams (Are Made of This)." With Reznor acting as a producer and co-writer, Manson went on to release the album *Antichrist Superstar* in 1996. The title, it turned out, was apt: fueled by the hit "The Beautiful People," Manson was launched into superstardom. Taking inspiration from shock rockers like Alice Cooper, Manson was as talented at creating controversy as he was writing music. Most famously, he was scapegoated for allegedly inspiring the 1999 Columbine massacre, during which two students killed scores of their peers before taking their own lives. Meanwhile, former Nine Inch Nails guitarist Richard Patrick launched his own project, Filter, and found success with the oh-so-'90s anthem "Hey Man, Nice Shot."

The popularity of Reznor and Manson's work was bound to inspire a wave of mostly terrible copycats, which it did, in the form of bands like Static-X and Orgy. More surprising, though, was the number of glam bands that desperately clung to their remaining fame by transitioning into industrial; it's possible the hair-metallers thought they'd fit in with the industrial bands because they shared horrible taste in fashion. Glam bands that attempted to evolve into industrial acts include Guns N' Roses, Mötley Crüe, Faster Pussycat, and L.A. Guns. Glam bands that successfully evolved into industrial acts do not exist.

In recent years, industrial has seen a small resurgence, largely thanks to projects like Youth Code. In any case, incorporating electronic elements into metal is wholly commonplace today. To paraphrase Nine Inch Nails, the lines between genres have blurred.

Extra Credit

1. **GODFLESH, "LIKE RATS"**
(Streetcleaner, 1989)

2. **MINISTRY, "JUST ONE FIX"**
(Psalm 69, 1992)

3. **NINE INCH NAILS, "LAST"**
(Broken, 1992)

4. **MARILYN MANSON, "THE BEAUTIFUL PEOPLE"**
(Antichrist Superstar, 1996)

5. **RAMMSTEIN, "DU HAST"**
(Sehnsucht, 1997)

Rammstein burning up San Jose, California, September 28, 2001.

8

Nu Metal

WHAT IS IT?

Effectively punchy riffs and biomechanical industrial mixed with weak white-boy rap.

WHO LISTENS TO IT?

Anne Rice fans who work out in order to be intimidating and do designer drugs as a license to feel bad.

WHERE DOES IT COME FROM?

California, mostly, but occasionally Iowa.

BASTARD CHILDREN:

Rap metal, mall goth, aggro, disco metal, jock metal, thugcore.

THE BIG FOUR:

Korn, Limp Bizkit, Linkin Park, and Slipknot.

Coal Chamber, probably smelling just wonderful, 2000.

ecause heavy metal is loud, audacious, and often involves lyrics about Dracula, the outside world considers it immature. According to your average music fan, you should outgrow heavy metal once you're old enough to pay a utility bill. Within the metal universe, though, the most immature genre is nu metal.

This is interesting, given that nu metal occurred somewhat far into metal's existence, and was preceded by everyone from Iron Maiden to Cannibal Corpse. But you only need to observe a shift in hand gestures to understand how nu metal changed the game. Throughout heavy metal's existence, the official sign of membership into the fold has been the Devil Horns, or what purists call "The Goat"—index finger and pinkie extended, middle and ring fingers down, thumbs tucked.[1] But for nu-metallers, concepts like sex, drugs, violence, and the Devil had been worn out by the metalheads of the past, who'd turned into dads with jobs. The burgeoning misfits of the day realized that the open-mouthed horror these things instilled in normal folks mattered more than the values themselves. So, instead of throwing the horns, nu metal fans gave everyone the finger. Instead of saying they worshipped Satan or killed babies, they said "fuck." And it worked. Teachers were pissed.

Like the shock value its makers court, nu metal is all about punch. The instrumental mastery of Iron Maiden just didn't cut it in '94; these kids had grown up on thousand-ton Pantera riffs and bass

[1] The horns without the thumb tucked is the second-falsest gesture a metalhead can make, topped only by the thumb-and-pinkie-extended Hang Ten. Both of these will earn you smug disdain at heavy metal shows, but as with all of the territorial trappings of heavy metal, none of this really fucking matters.

Coal Chamber smelling considerably more like sandalwood a few years later.

drops in hip-hop and techno beats. Perhaps this is why, as their sword of choice, nu-metal musicians went for the seven-string guitar—an electric guitar with one extra string on the bass end that gives chords a percussive impact perfect for a 4/4 dance beat. The seven-string makes every second of every song a kinetic experience—one you can feel from your teeth to your ass. It's loud, rude, and sexy.

"It was Fear Factory who originally used that tuning," says Dez Fafara, former frontman for nu-metal heavyweights Coal Chamber. Mixing crushing riffs with Tim Burton–ish goth, Coal Chamber helped build the spooky foundation on which nu metal was built. "The L.A. scene was really dead at the time—the hair-metal scene had completely died, and clubs were dying out. A lot of bands were coming up at the time. Incubus weren't anything like the white-bread, milquetoast pop band they are now—they were actually a heavy-metal act. We weren't calling it anything, we just knew that it was something different."

Drugs helped. The drugs of the early 2000s were dangerous and scientific—E, crack, meth, and any number of science class substances like GHB or Vicodin. The possibility of addiction and overdose

added to the self-harming shock factor of the music. In that way, and in many others, nu metal was a reiteration of glam (page 63). Like glam, it was driven by hard-hitting and catchy sounds that made hips sway and grind. Like glam, it played with gender roles and substance abuse. And, like glam, youth was its defining trait, so that a band's cred was determined by just how terribly its lyrics ruined Thanksgiving.

The difference was that glam was all about sexy street grit and Hollywood dreams, with its roots buried in working-class white culture. Nu metal, meanwhile, was surrounded by the rising scenes of grunge and gangsta rap. The former was caught up in the confusion and angst of being a genuine human being; the latter dealt with the too-real trauma of being poor and discriminated against, and living a life of crime. Nu metal ate it up, even if it couldn't walk the walk.

"I was never in love with Pearl Jam or Nirvana," says Fafara. "I see their worth, but I was never part of that scene. In order to keep the scene alive, we all just dove into our influences. We liked heavy stuff, and that's what we were going to do. It was really L.A. versus Seattle."

Soulfly's Max Cavalera needs a TUMS, circa 2000.

SHOW US ON THE DOLL

Nu metal's sound developed in a relatively short time frame. Several bands informed the genre, primarily a handful of unclassifiable acts out of California. The Red Hot Chili Peppers blended everything from punk to classic rock to reggae, making music about addiction and depression that somehow remained upbeat and catchy. Long Beach crew Sublime impressed a new generation of potheads with its laid-back tales of strife-ridden gangbanger life.

Thrash metal's young talents even tried their hand. Sepultura's 1996 release, *Roots,* is a burly, seven-string nightmare, and after his fraught departure from the band that year, frontman Max Cavalera started Soulfly, whose modern primitive

Rage Against the Machine, circa 1991.

rage against the machine

imagery inspired a whole generation of metalheads to get tribal tattoos. Bay Area thrash crew Machine Head also took part, with frontman and Slayer favorite Robb Flynn replacing his ragged hair and sleeveless T-shirt with liberty spikes and a track suit. Alt-metal nutcases Faith No More also showed off the effectiveness of mixing pointedly heavy riffs with cartoonish insanity—all with a considerable dose of funk bounce (see A Crash Course in Alternative Metal, page 117).

Perhaps the most noble of the bands that could be called nu metal was Los Angeles's Rage Against the Machine. While nu metal was often plagued with overly simplistic riffs and clumsy rhymes, RATM's musicianship was genuinely impressive. Frontman Zack de la Rocha's lyrics were intelligent and creative, and lead guitarist Tom Morello was a technical genius. It helped that de la Rocha rapped about social-justice issues rather than sickness and anger, penning rabid hard-rock tunes about police brutality ("Killing in the Name Of"), gang corruption ("Bulls on Parade"), and the hypocrisy of the media ("Guerilla Radio"). The band's first three albums have survived the nu-metal era somewhat spotlessly.

But every form of art has an epitomizing artist: the person or people that encapsulate everything it's about. For nu metal, that will always be Korn, from Bakersfield, California.

The proper spelling of Korn's name is capital *K*, lowercase *O*, backward capital *R*, lowercase *N*. The stylization suggests a twisted childhood innocence, which is the primary theme of Korn's music. This is also displayed in the band's album covers, most notably that of its debut, where a schoolgirl on a playground swing tries to block the sun in her eyes in order to see a lank figure throwing a menacing

Korn live in 1998. Guess which one of the mannequins is full.

shadow. On the back of the CD, girl and shadow are gone. It is implied that, later, a cop will hand some wide-eyed mother a soiled pink sneaker.

Korn's music drips with anguish, disillusionment, and reactionary rage. Guitarists Brian "Head" Welch and James "Munky" Shaffer alternate between dissonant chords and combative riffs. Reginald "Fieldy" Arvizu's rattling slap bass pairs perfectly with David Silveria's steady nightclub drums. Combining with them all are the vocals of Jonathan Davis, a dreadlocked frontman whose mixture of gibbering, barking, and childish keening makes the listener think of a teenage runaway who was loved in all the wrong ways.

The merging of these aspects tapped into the emotional constipation of middle-class teenagers whose own fury and angst were being overlooked as First World Problems. Like the glam bands before it, Korn was all about being fucked up and crazy; unlike Mötley Crüe and W.A.S.P., Korn's drug-fueled antics were born out of pain rather than ego. In a *Rolling Stone* article about the creation of the band's first album, Davis describes how the recording of "Ball Tongue" was fueled entirely by crystal meth:

Went to my dealer and got a big ol' fat rock of meth, chopped that shit up and I did vocals. "Ball Tongue" was about our close friend and kind of manager, from Huntington. That was his nickname, because when he was tweaking, he'd just sort of seize up and his tongue was like a ball. All that crazy, scatting shit, that was all from me probably being up too long.

While Korn's self-titled debut was an instant underground classic and the gothier tones of 1996's *Life Is Peachy* solidified the band's sound, none of the band's previous releases—and none of its later ones—compared to 1998's *Follow the Leader.* Featuring a cover by comic-book artists Todd Macfarlane and Greg Capullo (best known for their work on Macfarlane's groundbreaking series *Spawn*) and guest appearances by Ice Cube and the Pharcyde's Tre Hardson, *Follow the Leader* showed the world that Korn's misery-riddled music couldn't be ignored any longer.

The videos for *Follow*'s two big singles, "Got the Life" and "Freak on a Leash," dominated MTV soon after the album's release. "Got the Life" showed the grimy-looking dudes in the band enjoying a rock-star lifestyle normally reserved for pretty people, while "Freak" followed a bullet zooming around L.A. and destroying all it came in contact with while the band performed in a wooden shack. The latter became an anthem for out-of-place teens everywhere.

Despite selling millions of albums and appearing on every horror-movie soundtrack released after 1997, Korn has remained somewhat of a respected staple of the metal scene. The band spat in the face of commercial success even as it won it; when the group became known for its love of sports brand Adidas, Davis wrote a song where the name became an acronym for "All Day I Dream About Sex." Even as Davis went on to score movies, Welch kicked heroin and found Christ, and Fieldy released two abysmal gangsta-rap albums, the band stayed true to its ghetto-goth sound, releasing one album after another about unstable latchkey kids trying to piece together their awful lives.

Kid Rock, in December 2001, playing for the troops at Ramstein Air Base, Germany.

BIG PANTS, BIGGER ASSHOLES

While Korn introduced nu metal into the mainstream, its level of inner darkness was marginalizing for some. To truly explode, nu metal needed a band that was geared less toward broken dolls and more toward the average straight, white high-school male.

That band was Limp Bizkit, a polished rap-rock sextet from Jacksonville, Florida, that traded Korn's haunted house dysfunction for prep-school gangster bravado. Led by baby-faced tattoo artist Fred Durst, Limp Bizkit was nu metal at its poppiest—riffs so simple they were stupid, high-pitched rhymes about bitches, and catchy choruses you can scream while bouncing on the balls of your feet. The band's first big single was a cover of George Michael's "Faith," which was soon followed by "Nookie," in which a female antagonist is urged to stick a cookie up her ass.

While Korn embodied nu metal's sound, Limp Bizkit embodied its pop-culture image. The band included DJ Lethal, known for his work with "Jump Around" scribes House of Pain, but all he did was scratch a record between the first and second verse of every song. Guitarist Wes Borland wore black contacts and painted himself like a giant voodoo doll, but in real life he was just a typical metal bro (Borland is in many ways the tragic figure of the band, a relatively talented guitarist consigned to playing the same dumb riffs over and over). The

BWAAAAAAAHAHAHAHAHA, AHA, AHA, AAAAAAAAAAAAHAHAHAHA!

Godsmack pose for a PSA about the dangers of navel tattoos, July 2001.

video for "Nookie" features a line of backup dancers dressed in Durst's signature khakis and red backward cap; the video ends with the band being arrested by the police, which is supposed to suggest criminality but instead feels like a reference to *Monty Python and the Holy Grail*.

If any band ruined nu metal, it was Limp Bizkit. Its lack of nuance made its anger smack of misogyny and suburban privilege. During a set at the ill-fated Woodstock '99 festival, a crowd of 200,000 fans went ape-shit and several sexual assaults were later reported, though it is worth noting that claims of Durst urging on the attackers are untrue. The average Limp Bizkit listener was quickly determined to be a white kid who'd never heard an actual metal band or rapper, and who aspired to be a weed dealer for the rich kids.

On top of that, the band ushered in an era of over-engineered, marketably angsty acts merging baby-proofed metal riffs and laughable rap. Papa Roach took over the airwaves with "Last Resort," a nu-metal anthem with shades of pop-punk known for its opening lines, "Cut my life into pieces / This is my last resort." Detroit rapper and former Vanilla Ice lookalike Kid Rock took on a trashy

redneck persona and became a radio sensation with "I Am the Bullgod" and "Bawitaba" (famous for the droning baby talk of its intro). Vanilla Ice himself revamped his image and put out an album recorded by nu-metal producer extraordinaire Ross Robinson. L.A. rap-rock outfit Crazy Town released "Butterfly," nu metal's attempt at a ballad, which inspired a million drunken ankle tattoos. In 2001, Dallas's Drowning Pool released "Bodies," arguably the dumbest and most overused hard-rock song of all time, in which the band members revealed that they could count to four.

As with death metal, those bands that added their own unique flavors to the formula were respected in their own right. Godsmack and Sevendust both made entertaining music, aided by unique frontmen, Wiccan biker Sully Erna and soulful life coach Lajon Witherspoon, respectively. Static-X, led by hyperactive toothbrush Wayne Static, fused cybergoth industrial with aggro riffs to create what was briefly dubbed "disco metal," a style also chugged out by Powerman 5000, whose members dressed like astronauts sponsored by Hot Topic and were led by Rob Zombie's little brother.

Better to reign in Iowa! Slipknot in 1999.

NINE GUYS, ONE CUP.

By 1998, record companies were scanning the globe for any band that had three dudes with piercings, a woman with metallic red hair, and a DJ.

Meanwhile, in Des Moines, Iowa, truly wretched shit was happening.

At first glance, Slipknot was a hive mind of gimmicks—nine guys in red jumpsuits and drugstore Halloween masks, assigned numbers between 0 and 8, including two alternate percussionists, a DJ, and a "samples guy." But as Rule #5 of Metal states (see page 8), the music is what matters, and Slipknot's amalgamated influences, personal issues, and shitty experiences

in Heartland America spawned an unstoppable juggernaut of metallic punishment.

Slipknot sounds like what comes out of a boil on death metal's neck: a primordial stew with all the hope and happiness of a prenatal deformity. It seems utterly reasonable that nine members are necessary to make music this unhinged. Slipknot requires it all—the frantic DJ'ing of Sid Wilson (#0), the droning bass of Paul Gray (#2), the serial-killer sleep talk of Craig Jones (#5), the misanthropic riffs of Mick Thompson and Jim Root (#7 and #4), the dynamic drumming of Joey Jordison (#1), the keg-assaulting backing rhythms of Chris Fehn (#3), the inexhaustible roar of Corey

Taylor (#8), and the seething mania of Shawn Crahan, a.k.a. Clown (#6 with a bullet).

Slipknot acted more like a Norwegian black-metal band than any L.A. wannabes. Fehn and Wilson were known for physically attacking each other throughout live performances. Crahan kept a dead crow in a jar and would huff its fumes pre-show, filling his mask with vomit; when he was feeling generous, he would hold the jar out to his fans, affectionately called "maggots." With the music to back them up, the jumpsuits and masks took on a sinister meaning—while other bands idolized Satan and the Marquis de Sade, Slipknot was nine dudes who grew up on Michael Myers and Jason Voorhees, unstoppable killing machines whose simple work clothes hid beneath them the nauseating madness of small-town America.

The first half of Slipknot's self-titled debut is still very much nu metal—Taylor sounds young and snotty, his voice polished and bright as he raps and sings in "Spit It Out." But the second half of the album is a murky horror-scape of pessimism and festering sexual frustration. And while many nu-metal bands used their second albums to refine their music into money-making radio fare, Slipknot's sophomore release, 2001's *Iowa*, saw the band trading its red jumpsuits for black ones and doubling down on the brutality. *Iowa* runs thick with blast-beats and tremolo picking, and Taylor's lyrics are puked poetry that confront Satanism . . . but only in how it was practiced by your average misanthropic hick. As Taylor puts it in

"The Heretic Anthem," "Nobody wants anything I've got, which is fine because you're made of everything I'm not!"

Iowa saved Slipknot from death by cliché. The band's dedication to crushing metal over passing trends forced even underground fans to begrudgingly accept them. The many cathartic side projects of its members—Taylor and Root's commercially successful rock group Stone Sour and Jordison's oddly satisfying horror punk crew Murderdolls—made sure that Slipknot's wounds stayed perpetually irritated and angry. While Gray's tragic death of a drug overdose and Jordison's departure in 2013 fractured the band somewhat, it has remained active, powerful, and super-fucking-scary.

Chino: not just a pants brand. Deftones, circa 1998.

YOU DON'T HAVE TO BE CRAZY TO WORK HERE . . .

As the twentieth century progressed into the twenty-first and nu metal went from musical phenomenon to cultural staple, certain bands attempted to set themselves apart from the pack. Mudvayne wore stylized face paint and made music similar to Slipknot's, but soon traded traditional aggro for crunchy math-metal that impressed even hardened headbangers. Evanescence, a band from Little Rock, Arkansas, led by songwriting pro Ben Moody and soaring vocalist Amy Lee, topped charts with its sweeping and romantic debut, *Fallen*. Chicago's Disturbed made ultra-polished groove metal about being crazy with massive success. Its debut, *The Sickness*, was also

Marilyn Mans— sorry, Amy Lee of Evanescence on the Nintendo Fusion Tour, California, August 24, 2003.

hugely popular, in part because of frontman David Draiman's distinct, barking battle cry (say it with me, now: "OOOO-WAH-AH-AH-AH!"). Somehow, the band's albums have become classics for a specific kind of metal fan (not to mention military personnel, who adore the band).

Two bands that paid their dues in nu metal evolved into respected game-changers. System of a Down was a madcap group of Armenian immigrants from Glendale, California, whose soulful music struck a chord with all rock fans. Its sophomore album, *Toxicity*, was lauded for its socially conscious themes and its unorthodox mixture of influences. Deftones, on the other hand, took pained riff rock and added a heroin-y dreaminess to it, the resulting music channeling unique atmosphere and genuine heart. Goateed frontman Chino Moreno intelligently gave up on rapping for a sort of tender crowing, and the band has continued making

anticipated albums to this day.

Perhaps the most successful nu-metal band of all time seemed like a total stereotype. Linkin Park featured a DJ and two vocalists, one of whom was a rapper and one of whom was named Chester. Its breakthrough single, "One Step Closer," had a teeter-totter rhythm and angsty lyrics; the crux of the song's music video was ninjas dancing on the ceiling. The band's debut album, *Hybrid Theory*, blew up in 2001—the year that nu metal caught a glimpse of itself in the mirror and shuddered.

Everyone thought the band would shine and burn out. Instead, Linkin Park defied nu-metal conventions and kept climbing. Its sound progressed, getting leaner and faster, brimming with inspirational lyrics and epic crescendos that only made Mike Shinoda's rhymes (he's the rapper) and Chester Bennington's lyrics seem genuine. In 2003, the band dropped *Meteora*, which

Linkin Park, nu metal's least crazy band, suggests craziness in Las Vegas, January 10, 2014.

featured a matured sense of musicianship and one infectious single after another. The videos for these songs were thoughtful and gorgeous, including a mesmerizing animated film for "Breaking the Habit" and a brilliantly choreographed video for "Faint." The next year, the band made a collaborative album with rapper Jay-Z, thus solidifying Linkin Park as the biggest rock band in the universe. It has since sold seventy million albums. Seventy. Million. Albums.

Linkin Park survived because the music came first for them. The band's career is almost disappointingly uncontroversial. No one died. No one made a racist comment outside of a nightclub. Bennington had issues with drinking and drugs, but according to an interview Shinoda did for *The Pulse of Radio*, the band dealt with it like a well-adjusted family:

> **When Chester had some problems, everybody jumped up to help him and tell him how supportive we wanted to be and how much it means to us that he was doing something positive. We're lucky to have a band full of guys who have their heads screwed on straight. A lot of life experience goes into that.... At the end of the day we love what we do. We're not willing to throw that away on anything.**

And yet, Linkin Park's lack of posturing might have been a warning of their very real issues. In July of 2017, Bennington hanged himself, leaving behind six children and stunned fans. His death was a chilling reminder even those who seem well-adjusted could still be hiding the scariest demons.

OH GOD, WHAT HAVE WE DONE?

"I hope you tell it like it really happened, man," says Fafara. "I hope you get what we were trying to do. We saved L.A., man."

Given its narcotics obsession, it's only fitting that nu metal ended like a drug trip—one day, everyone sort of woke up on the beach, saw what they were wearing, and bailed. Unlike grunge's perceived execution of glam (see Glam Metal, page 63), there was no song or era that killed nu metal. But it died. It died hard.

September 11, 2001, certainly didn't help. On the day Slayer released *God Hates Us All*, the United States was rocked by one of the worst domestic terror attacks in history. Suddenly, consumable hard-rock tunes about the problems of white suburbanites didn't seem very appropriate, or relevant. The bands with unique attitudes and musical integrity managed to hold on to their fan bases, but most of the chaff was cast aside. The mid-2010s saw an alleged nu-metal revival, though it was celebrated more by the press than anyone else.

And, besides, the underground was bubbling to the surface. Every other form of heavy metal had been lumped together in the same pit, and the communities were crossbreeding. Fans were being raised on everything from Dio to Deicide to Dissection. And as nu metal slowly ate itself to death, something loud and hairy and fun was emerging from the basement in a sleeveless black T-shirt . . . and it had a song to play you.

Starter Kit

Ready to jump da fuck up? You'll need:

- [ ] ONE (1) PAIR JNCO JEANS, THE BIGGER THE BETTER

- [ ] ONE (1) CANVAS BELT BY A SKATEBOARD MANUFACTURER, PREFERABLY MENACE OR ELEMENTAL

- [ ] FIVE (5) BALL-CHAIN NECKLACES, WORN ON NECK, WRISTS, AND HAT

- [ ] AT LEAST THREE (3) PIERCINGS IN YOUR EYEBROW AND/OR LIP

- [ ] 8 OZ. MANIC PANIC HAIR DYE, BLUE OR RED

- [ ] A DRUG DEALER'S BEEPER NUMBER

- [ ] SELF-INFLICTED WOUNDS

Homework

1. KORN, "BLIND"
(Korn, 1994)

2. RAGE AGAINST THE MACHINE, "KILLING IN THE NAME OF"
(Rage Against the Machine, 1992)

3. SOULFLY, "JUMPDAFUCKUP"
(Primitive, 2000)

4. GODSMACK, "WHATEVER"
(Godsmack, 1998)

5. COAL CHAMBER, "LOCO"
(Coal Chamber, 1997)

6. DEFTONES, "MY OWN SUMMER (SHOVE IT)"
(Deftones, 1997)

7. KID ROCK, "I AM THE BULLGOD"
(Devil Without a Cause, 1998)

8. MACHINE HEAD, "FROM THIS DAY"
(The Burning Red, 2000)

9. KORN, "GOT THE LIFE"
(Follow the Leader, 1998)

10. LIMP BIZKIT, "NOOKIE"
(Significant Other, 1999)

11. STATIC-X, "I'M WITH STUPID"
(Wisconsin Death Trip, 2000)

12. SLIPKNOT, "SURFACING"
(Slipknot, 1999)

13. SEVENDUST, "DENIAL"
(Home, 1999)

14. PAPA ROACH, "MY LAST RESORT"
(Infest, 2000)

15. DROWNING POOL, "BODIES"
(Sinner, 2001)

16. DISTURBED, "DOWN WITH THE SICKNESS"
(The Sickness, 2000)

17. DOPE, "KIMBERLY'S GHOST"
(Felons and Revolutionaries, 1999)

18. POWERMAN 5000, "SUPERNOVA GOES POP"
(Tonight the Stars Revolt, 1999)

19. THE UNION UNDERGROUND, "SOUTH TEXAS DEATHRIDE"
(. . . An Education in Rebellion, 2000)

20. SLIPKNOT, "THE HERETIC ANTHEM"
(Iowa, 2011)

21. SYSTEM OF A DOWN, "SCIENCE"
(Toxicity, 2001)

22. MUDVAYNE, "DIG"
(L.D. 50, 2000)

23. EVANESCENCE, "TAKING OVER ME"
(Fallen, 2003)

24. LINKIN PARK, "FAINT"
(Meteora, 2003)

Manowar dressed for prom night, October 1984.

A Crash Course in Power Metal

The easy description of power metal is: What would have happened if the New Wave of British Heavy Metal had never stopped? But that's inaccurate; though power metal is primarily defined by NWOBHM's instrumental grandstanding and romantic subject matter ("romantic" like medieval chivalry, not like the paperbacks your mom reads), thrash's speed and death metal's Viking battle lust heavily informed its sound, making it the often-mocked and self-reliant subgenre it currently is.

Yngwie Malmsteen (né Lars Johan Yngve Lannerbäck) is both power metal's forefather and an apt metaphor for the whole genre. Malmsteen grew up on a mixture of European proto-metal and classical violinist Nioccoló Paganini, and became known for his innovative style, including a form of speedy chugging eventually dubbed "shredding" that became the basis of power metal's guitar sound. However, while Malmsteen's debut solo album, *Rising Force*, is considered a metal must-have, the guy was just never a good songwriter. It is telling that Malmsteen has publicly stated that he was in no way influenced by Jimi Hendrix—there's nothing cool or sexy about his music (unlike that of former Hendrix roadie Lemmy, who was nothing but cool sex). At the end of the day, that's what power metal is—music of incredible talent and pure dedication that has to work hard not to suck.

Manowar holds the Guinness World Record for "Loudest Performance" and popularized the metalhead credo "Death to false metal." Manowar's music is hard-hitting and straightforward, mixing biker sensibilities with galloping anthems about ancient Norse warfare and dark wizardry. The band also considers being a metalhead a badge of honor, and references metal in its music constantly (in "Warriors of the World United," singer Eric Adams cries, "Stand and fight together beneath the metal sky," whatever that means).

Manowar's complete loyalty to old-school metalheaddom spawned generations of musicians who'd shun partying and Satanism and focus on instrumental prowess and old-school masculinity; it also stunted a million

Yngwie Malmsteen unleashes the fury (Google it), 1984.

Iced Earth, metal's answers to Ken Burns and *The Simpsons'* Comic Book Guy.

male emotions with clumsy misogyny, as in "Hail and Kill," when Adams wishes the listener, "May your sword stay wet, like a young girl in her prime." Gross.

When grunge took over from metal as the hairiest rock in town in the '90s, lots of metal subgenres sullenly shuffled underground. But power metal was used to being cast aside, and unlike other metal subgenres it was uninterested in digging a niche for itself or adopting the radio-safe term "hard rock." This unabashed respect for its roots endeared power metal to extreme metalheads, especially those in Europe, where grunge had not been the seismic shift it had been in the United States.

While Mötley Crüe was putting out industrially tinged garbage like *Generation Swine*, the dragon-enamored Rhapsody and the hammer-obsessed Hammerfall were headlining massive European festivals. Heavy-hitters Blind Guardian soon dominated the scene with its ambitious albums about J. R. R. Tolkien and goblins going to the opera. The Netherlands gave the world Epica, which had surprisingly mainstream appeal outside of North America, while Tampa, Florida, produced Kamelot, a romantic band with a massive female fan base.

The United States still had its stars, though, particularly Iced Earth, a Floridian band led by single-minded guitarist Jon Schaffer. What set

Iced Earth apart from the rest was a distinct American sensibility—a hint of swagger in the riffs, a touch of soul in the vocals, a gallop that felt more Clint Eastwood than Beowulf. Schaffer didn't write about hobbits and knights; he wrote about movie monsters, civil-war heroes, and comic books (the band's 1996 album *The Dark Saga* is based on Todd Macfarlane's *Spawn*, a comic series normally associated with nu metal). Because of this, Iced Earth thrived while other shredders were floundering, and Schaffer remains one of metal's more respected talents.

Having survived the '90s, power metal began to attract new followers. London's

Dragonforce is known for its video game-ish hyper-speed style and masturbatory three-minute solos, though it's as much a novelty act as a respectable band. Europe continues to produce over-the-top groups like Battle Beast and Axxis, while North America's modern contributions are a bit thrashier than not, with California's Holy Grail and Canada's Skull Fist bringing more shred than shimmer.

As metal subgenres become more disparate, fans continue to flock to power metal as a place to hear the music at its purest. This is the only explanation for its fans multiplying, as one observing the typical power metal crowd might question whether anyone they see will ever get laid in their lifetime.

Nice try, Dragonforce. Circa 2006.

Extra Credit

1. YNGWIE MALMSTEEN, "NOW YOUR SHIPS ARE BURNED"
(Rising Force, 1985)

2. MANOWAR, "BROTHERS OF METAL PT. 1"
(Louder Than Hell, 1996)

3. BLIND GUARDIAN, "BATTLEFIELD"
(A Night at the Opera, 2002)

4. ICED EARTH, "DRACULA"
(Horror Show, 2001)

5. SKULL FIST, "BAD FOR GOOD"
(Chasing the Dream, 2014)

9
Metalcore

(Or, The New Wave of American Heavy Metal)

WHAT IS IT?

An amalgamation of metal and hardcore.

WHO LISTENS TO IT?

People who don't want other people to know they feel all the feelings.

WHERE DOES IT COME FROM?

Seriously?

BASTARD CHILDREN:

Swedecore, mathcore, screamo, scenecore, crabcore.

THE BIG FOUR:

Lamb of God, Mastodon, Killswitch Engage, Shadows Fall.

Killswitch Engage shows are no laughing matter. August 23, 2006.

etal, like most art forms, is reactionary. After years of nu metal, it was inevitable that a more technically skilled format would eventually rise in popularity once again.

Still, when Massachusetts's Killswitch Engage released its 2002 breakthrough album, *Alive or Just Breathing*, it had no idea how prophetic the title of opening track "Numbered Days" would be.

Asked if he realized at the time that the song's chorus—"Kingdoms will rise to power, but kingdoms fall to dust"—would be a perfect metaphor for the relationship between nu metal and metalcore, vocalist Jesse Leach responds with an emphatic, "No! I was in no way thinking that or even in a mindset of the end or beginning of any music genre. The song has various meanings; I think I just wanted it to sound apocalyptic and threatening."

But if any album announced the New Wave of American Heavy Metal's arrival, it was *Alive or Just Breathing*. When the band performed "Numbered Days" live, audiences didn't have to be instructed to scream "Kingdoms FALL!" along with Leach. "Numbered Days" isn't a song, it's an anthem, and *Alive or Just Breathing* isn't an album—it's a declaration of war.

What made *Alive or Just Breathing* feel so fresh was its appropriation of Swedish melodic death metal—specifically, 1995's *Slaughter of the Soul,* by Gothenburg's At the Gates. At the time, *Slaughter of the Soul* was severely underappreciated, leaving its style ripe for reinvention. Bands like Killswitch Engage and its fellow Massholes in Shadows Fall and Unearth, D.C.'s Darkest Hour, and San Diego's As I Lay Dying were some of the earliest

American adopters of the Gothenburg sound, which made expert use of harmonized guitars, blindingly fast double-bass drumming, and death-metal caterwauling that still managed to include intonation.

But these bands didn't simply steal from At the Gates; like a campfire story, the Gothenburg sound was embellished as it was passed down. These acts had come of age at a time when MTV's *Headbanger's Ball* and metal magazines like *Circus* would cover all subgenres side by side, despite their lack of commonalities. Suddenly it was okay to have short hair at a metal show or long hair at a hardcore show, and to love Megadeth and Mötley Crüe equally. Consequently, this new generation of American metallers threw many different ingredients into their Gothenburg stew to create something different. In particular, they often employed at least one, if not both, of two specific elements not readily found in At the Gates' music.

The first of these is known as "good cop/bad cop vocals." This style consisted of the frontman screaming the verses in a manner similar to that of death metal and/or hardcore vocalists before belting the chorus in a clean, dramatic fashion.

The second of these are called "breakdowns," defined by the always-scholarly Internet UrbanDictionary as "the most brutal section" of a song, "characterized by a beat much slower than the main verses and chorus of a song . . . and a chugging rhythm from the guitar."

Initially, this new crop of bands was dubbed the New Wave of American Heavy Metal. Eventually, however, these groups were increasingly labeled "metalcore," because (ready?) they melded metal and hardcore. Following a decade of whining about not getting enough hugs as a kid over repetitive, simple-minded riffs, metalcore was just the kick in the nards metal needed to stay vital.

EVERYBODY LOVES A LITTLE KSE

Alive or Just Breathing is actually KsE's second record, after a self-titled debut in 2000. But the album was, for all intents and purposes, a reboot of the band, and by the time its touring cycle was over, its lineup would undergo major transitions, thereby cementing what is arguably the "definitive" version of Killswitch Engage.

Specifically, those transitions were the departure of Leach and the decision to move Adam Dutkiewicz, who also produced KsE's albums, from drums to guitar (bassist/album cover designer Mike D'Antonio and guitarist Justin Stroetzel stayed put). The band auditioned multiple possible replacements for Leach, including Phil Labonte, the All That Remains vocalist who had also once been a member of Shadows Fall. They wisely[1] settled on Howard Jones, the muscular, African-American frontman for Connecticut's Blood Has Been Shed (as well as Blood Has Been Shed's drummer, Justin Foley).

Some disliked Adam D.'s stage presence, which is a deliberately goofy "fuck you" to metal machismo (he often sports a cape and cutoff jean shorts). But no one really took this criticism seriously, and Killswitch Engage soon became metal's "next big thing."

In 2004, Killswitch Engage made good on that hype with the release of *The End of Heartache*, its first album with the new roster. Jones's clean vocals were even more soulful and soaring than those of Leach. Furthermore, Leach generally wrote lyrics dealing with such lofty topics as politics, philosophy, and spirituality; Jones, an avowed fan of the popular goth outfit HIM, just as often wrote about broken hearts.

The End of Heartache's standout, in fact, was its title track. In addition to having an insanely strong hook, the song included so few "bad cop" vocals that the band was able to release a scream-free version for a *Resident Evil* movie soundtrack. "Heartache" was ostensibly metalcore's answer to the power ballad. In no time, Killswitch Engage was headlining venues ten times the size the ones the band been playing just a couple of years prior.

KsE made two more albums with Jones. The first, 2006's *As Daylight Dies*, was well-received and spawned two hits: another pseudo-power ballad, "The End of Sorrow"; and a cover Dio's most famous song, "Holy Diver," complete with a delightfully silly video parodying Dio's original clip. Fans were not happy with 2009's *Killswitch Engage*. The album was the band's first—and, to date, last—on which Dutkiewicz had a co-producer: Brendan O'Brien, best known for his work with decidedly more mainstream bands like Aerosmith and Pearl Jam. The announcement made fans fear a watered-down Killswitch Engage, and, unfortunately, those fears were not unfounded.

In the years following *Killswitch Engage*'s release, Jones was plagued by scandalous rumors of personal improprieties. He would later admit that he had been diagnosed with diabetes and was struggling with depression. In 2012, he left the band, telling fans in a statement that "my heart wasn't in it" anymore.

Rumors that the band would either recruit Labonte or reunite with Leach spread like wildfire. Fortunately,[2] the band chose the latter option. As of this writing, KsE has made two additional albums with Leach: 2013's *Disarm the Descent* and 2016's *Incarnate*. Both met with mostly positive reviews from fans and critics alike, even if it would be fair to say that neither duplicated the impact of *Alive or Just Breathing* or *The End of Heartache*. Still, Killswitch Engage's popularity is in no danger of dwindling anytime soon.

---

1 Labonte can't sing.

2 Labonte can't sing.

Lamb of God before the world gnawed on them hard.

CHURCH MUSIC

Two years before Killswitch Engage semi-reset with *Alive or Just Breathing*, a Virginia band called Burn the Priest did the same. Now rechristened Lamb of God, the quintet released its first album, *New American Gospel*, in 2000. The title was only slightly less prophetic than that of Killswitch Engage's "Numbered Days." Lamb of God would become one of the biggest metal bands of its generation.

Although it also melded metal and hardcore, Lamb of God's music was largely dissimilar to that of the band's Northeastern peers, being less rooted in the Gothenburg style. Instead, LoG stuck closer to its own geographic location for influences and sounded like the unholy lovechild of groove-metal bands like Pantera and Crowbar and sludgecore bands like Eyehategod, Acid Bath, and Soilent Green (see A Crash Course in Groove Metal and Sludge, page 172).

Lamb of God—along with fellow Pantera acolytes like New Jersey's God Forbid, Ohio's Chimaira, and California's DevilDriver—largely forewent good cop/bad cop vocals, singing only sparingly, if at all. These bands did not share Howard Jones's sense of romanticism; emerging right as George W. Bush was entering office, LoG and God Forbid mostly wrote about politics, while DevilDriver and Chimaira generally screamed about hating everyone.[3]

LoG was at the forefront of this other, heavier sphere of metalcore, and deservedly so. The band writes great songs. Drummer Chris Adler is what is popularly known in the industry as "a beast." The synchronized, syncopated attack of guitarists

---

3 In fact, the chorus to Chimaira's most famous song, "Pure Hatred," is "I. Hate. EVERYONE."

of Death," in which those in the crowd first split into two halves on opposite sides of the room and then charge at each other full force when the song really kicks off, like the opposing armies in *Braveheart*.

If Killswitch Engage was for young people who were angry because their feelings were hurt by a girl, Lamb of God was for young people who were angry because their feelings were hurt by the world. Unfortunately, on June 27, 2012, the world hurt these people again.

Immediately upon landing in Prague for a performance, Blythe, to his great surprise, was arrested for manslaughter. The charges stemmed from a show Lamb of God had played two years prior, at which a nineteen-year-old fan, Daniel Nosek, sustained injuries that would later kill him. Prosecutors alleged that these injuries resulted from Blythe having pushed Nosek off the stage and into the crowd—a common practice at extreme music shows, where the unwritten law is that stage divers need to cede their space back to the performers within seconds.

None of the band members had any recollection of the event. Indeed, the show in question had been uneventful. No one had ever informed Lamb of God of Nosek's injury or death, and for reasons that remain a mystery, the US State Department knew that Blythe was a wanted man in the Czech Republic, yet never bothered to inform him.

Blythe was held in Pankrác Prison, and faced up to ten years if convicted. He knew little

Mark Morton and Willie Adler (Chris's brother) and bassist John Campell is as tight and satisfying as any in metal. Morton, an avowed fan of Southern rock bands like the Black Crowes, plays his solos with a bluesy element more akin to Slash and Zakk Wylde than Jeff Hanneman and Marty Friedman. Frontman Randy Blythe is an intelligent, politically outspoken, highly charismatic focal point who happens to look like a rabid scarecrow onstage.

Lamb of God's public image was also in contrast with that of the KsEs of the world. There was no goofy joking around to be seen at a Lamb of God show. And, as if to drive home the point that this was an uncompromisingly brutal band, Lamb of God popularized something known as "The Wall

Czech, and few of his fellow inmates or prison administrators spoke English. Despite paying hundreds of thousands of dollars—no small amount for a working-class musician—prosecutors repeatedly appealed his attorneys' motion for bail, fearing he'd flee and never return for his trial, despite his assurances otherwise.

Blythe was finally released five weeks after his initial arrest. He flew home to the United States, where his wife and bandmates tearfully welcomed him back. True to his word, Blythe returned to Prague the following year to stand trial. He was acquitted on March 5, 2013, but his victory was bittersweet. Writing on Instagram on March 8,

Blythe said that, despite the verdict, "I am in no way shape or form a happy man right now," reminding fans that "a young man is still dead, & his family still suffers."

Lamb of God's 2015 release *VII: Sturm und Drang* includes a song, "512," named after the number of the Pankrác Prison cell in which Blythe slept. "My hands are painted red, my future's painted black," Blythe cries on the song, sounding at once incensed, terrified, and forlorn. Regardless of his innocence, it's clear that Nosek's death will continue to weigh heavily on Blythe for the rest of his life.

Lamb of God's Randy Blythe at Brixton Academy, London, January 18, 2014.

As I Lay Dying (with vocalist/shitbag Tim Lambesis, center), July 16, 2005.

AN EVEN BIGGER ASSHOLE THAN PHIL LABONTE

Still, this is not the most traumatic misfortune to ever befall a metalcore band.

As I Lay Dying came to its conclusion in 2013, when steroidal vocalist Tim Lambesis was arrested for attempting to hire an undercover cop to murder his estranged wife so as to secure custody of their adopted children. He was in jail until 2016. During that time, he attempted to sue the prison medical team for $35 million, alleging that it had failed to properly wean him off of steroids, resulting in gynecomastia, better known as "moobs" or "bitch tits." Almost immediately upon his release, Lambesis made plans to marry his extremely brave girlfriend.

Lambesis's AILD bandmates, meanwhile, wisely recruited a new singer and rebranded as Wovenwar.

MASTODDDAAAAAAMMMMNNN!!!

Meanwhile, in Atlanta, Georgia, a band called Mastodon was born. If At the Gates' influence was less noticeable on Lamb of God compared with Killswitch Engage and Darkest Hour, with Mastodon it was nonexistent. Put simply, Mastodon—bassist/vocalist Troy Sanders, guitarist/vocalist Brent Hinds, guitarist Bill Kelliher, and drummer Brann Dailor—has always been the oddball of NWOAHM. The band's debut album, *Remission* (2002), sounded filthier, more stripped-down, and proggier than most of the day's other popular releases. It was as though someone had taken Sabbath, the Melvins, Neurosis, Pink Floyd, and the Deaths (Napalm and regular), and shoved them into a hornet's nest, which they then hit with a stick.

Mastodon at the Scion Rock Fest in Atlanta, Georgia, February 28, 2009.

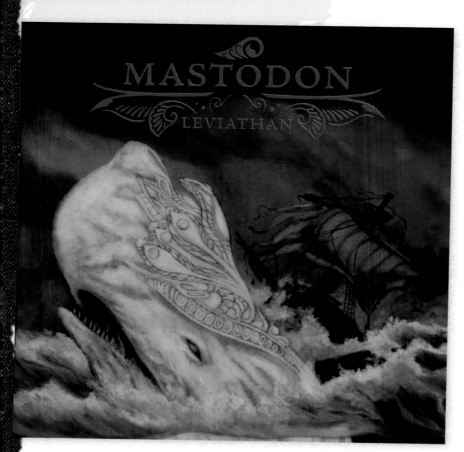

Despite the obvious hardcore influences on parts of *Leviathan*, Mastodon seemed out of place on tours with more straightforward metalcore bands like Trivium and As I Lay Dying. Regardless, *Leviathan* was very successful, and Mastodon also soon found itself signed to a major label, Reprise.

The band's first album under the new deal, 2006's *Blood Mountain*, is very much of a kind with *Remission* and *Leviathan*. But it also began a trend of each Mastodon album being less aggro than the one before it.

The evolution was gradual, but the Mastodon of today barely resembles the Mastodon of *Leviathan*, despite the band retaining all of its original members. On *Crack the Skye* (2009), *The Hunter* (2011), *Once More 'Round the Sun* (2014), and *Emperor of Sand* (2017), Mastodon is ostensibly a prog band with a hard-rock edge. Hinds even more-or-less disowned the band's metal roots in 2015, when he told *Guitar Player,* "I fucking hate heavy metal, and I don't want to be in a heavy metal band." He would later claim that he actually said, "I fucking hate most heavy metal," but listening to Mastodon's newer music, it's not hard to believe the initial quote's authenticity.

Despite this, Mastodon's popularity never waned. The metal community is like the mafia. Every time you think you're out, they pull you back in.

Remission got the metal world's attention, but what really put Mastodon on the map was 2004's *Leviathan*, a concept album inspired by Herman Melville's *Moby Dick*.

"Blood and Thunder," *Leviathan*'s opening track, begins with a single, twangy guitar playing the song's main riff before Dailor's drums explode like fireworks and the rest of the band kicks in. It's like a thrashier version of Nirvana's "Smells Like Teen Spirit." By the time they get to Clutch's Neil Fallon roaring the anthemic chorus—"WHITE! WHALE! HO-LY! GRAIL!"—listeners are either hooked or medically dead. Released as *Leviathan*'s lead single, "Blood and Thunder" was an announcement from Mastodon: "We are not the band with which you want to fuck."

Atreyu waiting for their moms to pick them up, circa 2005.

SHADOWS FALLEN AND THEY CAN'T GET UP

Mastodon and Lamb of God thrived on major labels, but some bands weren't so lucky. Two groups that took the leap but didn't stick the landing were Atreyu and the Shadows Fall. The latter is the more noteworthy of the two, because it was one of metalcore's earliest adopters, and for a time was thought to be one of metal's next massive A-List acts.

After parting ways with Phil Labonte over "creative differences,"[4] Shadows Fall recruited Brian Fair, an affable Rasta skater with massive dreadlocks that nearly touched the ground. Fair had previously roared for Overcast, a metalcore band that also featured future members of Killswitch Engage. The band began to shift its sound in a thrashier direction, and the hat trick of 2000's *Of One Blood*, 2002's *The Art of Balance*, and 2004's *The War Within* grabbed the metalsphere by the balls.

Shadows Fall signed with Atlantic Records for its next album, 2007's *Threads of Life*. Regrettably, it didn't connect with fans, presenting a version of Shadows Fall with much of its edge shaved down. The band had already covered "Teas'n, Pleas'n" by the Texas glam act Dangerous Toys, but on *Life* its members leaned into their love of hair metal hard. The album's most famous song is "Another Hero Lost," a ballad that could have been taken from a Skid Row record.

Shadows Fall may have felt that this strategy would work because it had worked for one of its

Either Avenged Sevenfold or a New Kids on the Block reunion, circa 2006.

peers: Avenged Sevenfold. That Orange County quartet made several inarguably metalcore albums before signing with Warner Bros. and shifting its sound toward the mainstream metal of the members' youth (Metallica, GN'R, etc.). The result, 2005's *City of Evil*, launched Avenged Sevenfold into the stratosphere. The band went on to release two albums that would debut at #1 on the Billboard 200: *Nightmare* (2010) and *Hail to the King* (2013).

But there's a massive difference between Shadows Fall and Avenged Sevenfold—the latter band had arena rock hardcoded into its DNA right from its inception. A7X has always pissed off metal purists, despite featuring excellent musicians and songwriters, because its members dress like Hot Topic catalog models and use stage names like "Synyster Gates" and "Zacky Vengeance." The band is, in the simplest terms, too silly in all the wrong ways for Slayer fans . . . but exactly the right kind of silly for Mötley Crüe fans. As such its metamorphosis into a more traditionally commercial-sounding band didn't alienate its core fan base.

But Shadows Fall was supposed to be a "real" metal band—and so *Threads of Life* didn't land with its audience. The band never made another album for Atlantic.

At least in terms of popularity, Shadows Fall never quite recovered from *Threads of Life*. The band announced that it was going on hiatus in 2014, and has only played the occasional show since. Meanwhile, its members have mostly moved on to other projects; most notably, lead guitarist Jon Donais was recruited by the revered thrash act Anthrax.

JANE DOE(S WHATEVER THE FUCK SHE WANTS)

While some metalcore bands chased the spotlight, others seemed to find it quite by accident.

Take, for example, Converge, from Salem, Massachusetts. Its brand of metalcore is distinct from that of a band like Shadows Fall. It's about as confrontational as confrontational gets, leaning largely on the speed and ferocity of punk. And yet, the band's fan base is substantial—and seemingly still growing after twenty-six years.

A perhaps even more unlikely success story is that of the Dillinger Escape Plan, from New Jersey. Anyone who heard the band's 1999 full-length debut, *Calculating Infinity*, had to admit that it was highly unique. But it's unlikely anyone would have guessed that the band would go on to open for Nine Inch Nails, make an EP with Faith No More's Mike Patton, perform on *Late Night with Conan O'Brien*, and still be around, more popular than ever, nearly twenty years later.

The reason most people might have underestimated the amount of success Dillinger would attain? Simple: its music—especially the early work—is really challenging to the listener.

Dillinger Escape Plan outside the Astoria in London, February 23, 2008.

THE DILLINGER ESCAPE PLAN

CALCULATING INFINITY

Trivium, featuring foreword-writer extraordinaire, Matt Heafy (second from the left), at Bloodstock Festival, England, 2015.

DEP specialize in a sub-subgenre of metalcore known as "mathcore." As the name suggests, mathcore amalgamates hardcore with metal at its most academic. The music of DEP and other mathcore bands is chaotic, angular, and avant-garde, the kind of stuff that challenges the mainstream's very definition of what "music" is. The band's performances are similarly anarchistic; the group's members are such skilled musicians that they're able to play incredibly complex pieces of music almost flawlessly while simultaneously performing acrobatic feats of daredevilry. They crowd surf, climb walls, hang perilously from monitors, leap from tall places they weren't supposed to be on in the first place, spit fire, break bones, and bleed all over the stage. Every Dillinger concert probably shaves a few years off their lives.

The popularity of bands like DEP and Converge speaks to the grassroots nature of extreme music. These bands got big because they were doing something unique, they were doing it well, and word spread organically. By the time Dillinger calmed down ever so slightly and started introducing elements of alternative and electronic music into its work, the band was already beyond reproach. The very small number of schmucks who ever dared cry "sellouts" were shouted down quickly and never heard from again.

Put another way: if Avenged Sevenfold and All That Remains were the guys who got the girls 'cause they drove really sweet cars, Converge and the Dillinger Escape Plan were the guys who got the girls because they appeared to have no interest whatsoever in getting the girls.

These two opposing approaches to metalcore still exist today. There are bands like Attack Attack! and Black Veil Brides, who bet big on arena rock hooks and Auto-Tune,[5] and there are bands like Norma Jean and Trap Them, who appear to make music for themselves first and an audience second. Whichever type of metalcore individual fans prefer, they can all agree on this: anything is better than nu metal.

---

5 Auto-Tune is a technology whereby vocals that are off-key can be corrected via computer. This is helpful for frontmen such as All That Remains' Phil Labonte, who can't sing.

Starter Kit

Ready to walk with me in hell? You will need:

- [ ] FACIAL HAIR THAT IS EITHER METICULOUSLY GROOMED OR NOT EVEN SLIGHTLY JUST A LITTLE BIT GROOMED

- [ ] ONE (1) T-SHIRT FOR A HARDCORE BAND YOU'VE NEVER ACTUALLY LISTENED TO

- [ ] ONE (1) T-SHIRT FOR A DEATH-METAL OR THRASH BAND YOU'VE NEVER ACTUALLY LISTENED TO

- [ ] ONE (1) "IRONIC" VINTAGE T-SHIRT FOR A HAIR-METAL BAND WHOSE CATALOGUE YOU KNOW BETTER THAN THE FACE OF YOUR OWN MOTHER

- [ ] ONE (1) BUTTON-DOWN SHIRT IN A DARK COLOR THAT IS NOT BLACK

- [ ] ONE (1) BAND HOODIE, BLACK

- [ ] ONE (1) PAIR SKATER SHOES, DESIGN OF YOUR CHOICE

- [ ] ONE (1) PAIR OF BLUE JEANS, RIPPED

- [ ] IN-DEPTH KNOWLEDGE OF AN ANIMATED CHILDREN'S PROGRAM FROM THE 1980S

- [ ] NO FEWER THAN TWO (2) BODY MODIFICATIONS THAT WOULD PRECLUDE YOU FROM HAVING A SO-CALLED "RESPECTABLE" JOB (E.G., FACIAL TATTOOS AND/OR PIERCINGS)

Homework

1. **KILLSWITCH ENGAGE, "NUMBERED DAYS"**

   (Alive or Just Breathing, 2002)

2. **LAMB OF GOD, "NOW YOU'VE GOT SOMETHING TO DIE FOR"**

   (Ashes of the Wake, 2004)

3. **MASTODON, "BLOOD AND THUNDER"**

   (Leviathan, 2004)

4. **SHADOWS FALL, "THE POWER OF I AND I"**

   (The War Within, 2004)

5. **DARKEST HOUR, "CONVALESCENCE"**

   (Undoing Ruin, 2005)

6. **GOD FORBID, "THE END OF THE WORLD"**

   (IV: Constitution of Treason, 2005)

7. **HATEBREED, "HEALING TO SUFFER AGAIN"**

   (Perseverance, 2002)

8. **UNEARTH, "THIS LYING WORLD"**

   (The Oncoming Storm, 2004)

9. **TRIVIUM, "PULL HARDER ON THE STRINGS OF YOUR MARTYR"**

   (Ascendency, 2005)

10. **AS I LAY DYING, "CONFINED"**

    (Shadows Are Security, 2005)

11. **CHIMAIRA, "PURE HATRED"**

    (The Impossibility of Reason, 2003)

12. **DEVILDRIVER, "GRINFUCKED"**

    (The Fury of Our Maker's Hand, 2005)

13. **A LIFE ONCE LOST, "VULTURE"**

    (Hunter, 2005)

14. **BURY YOUR DEAD, "HOUSE OF STRAW"**

    (Beauty and the Breakdown, 2006)

15. **ATREYU, "OUR SICK STORY (SO FAR)"**

    (A Deathgrip on Yesterday, 2006)

16. **ALL THAT REMAINS, "THE DEEPEST GRAY"**

    (This Darkened Heart, 2004)

17. **AVENGED SEVENFOLD, "BAT COUNTRY"**

    (City of Evil, 2005)

18. **EVERY TIME I DIE, "APOCALYPSE NOW AND THEN"**

    (Gutter Phenomenon, 2006)

19. **CONVERGE, "CONCUBINE"**

    (Jane Doe, 2001)

20. **THE DILLINGER ESCAPE PLAN, "43% BURNT"**

    (Calculating Infinity, 1999)

21. **BOTCH, "TRANSITIONS FROM PERSONA TO OBJECT"**

    (We Are the Romans, 1999)

22. **CAVE IN, "TERMINAL DEITY"**

    (Until Your Heart Stops, 1999)

23. **NORMA JEAN, "MEMPHIS WILL BE LAID TO WASTE"**

    (Bless the Martyr and Kiss the Child, 2002)

As I Lay Dying wows people at the Bloodstock Festival, England, in 2008.

Metal Criminals : In the Woods, There Is No Law

Since metal music often centers on behavior caused by the hasty consumption of a budget sixer, it's unsurprising that many metal musicians have criminal records. However, while many of their crimes are typical drunk-tank fare, certain artists have committed transgressions that will forever be a part of who they are. These are the real metal criminals: the ones whose music and illegal behavior go hand in hand.

For your sick pleasure, here's a short list of the metal world's most wanted, and the scandalous acts that got them in trouble with the law.

OZZY OSBOURNE

CHARGES: Assault, public intoxication, animal cruelty, public urination on the Alamo.

PUNISHMENT: Rough mornings in the drunk tank, banned from San Antonio for a decade.

While Ozzy's bad behavior often seems puckish and absurd—peeing on a national monument while wearing your wife's dress is pretty funny, and biting the heads off of doves and bats has a certain repulsive *je ne sais quoi*—the infamous night where he tried to choke his wife, Sharon, is distinctly menacing. Ozzy allegedly said, "We're very sorry, but you have to die," while trying to strangle her, which is about as

We call this "foreshadowing": Ozzy and Sharon Osbourne during the *Ultimate Sin* photoshoot, April 19, 1986.

terrifying a sentence as they come. Thankfully, the event helped set Ozzy straight—or at least straight enough not to publicly assault his family anymore.

Axl Rose under arrest at JFK in New York, July 12, 1992.

AXL ROSE

CHARGES: Public intoxication, battery, domestic abuse, biting a security guard's leg.

PUNISHMENT: Gaining fifty extra pounds, apparently.

Part of why Rose's bad-boy image resounded with metal fans was because there was truth behind it. Rose was arrested dozens of times in his hometown of Lafayette, Indiana, for crimes like public intoxication and battery. He was also later known for beating up his girlfriends, specifically Erin Everly and model Stephanie Seymour, during GN'R's heyday. His refusal to finish a set in St. Louis in 1991 caused a massive riot, which Rose was arrested for inciting. If that weren't enough, he bit a security guard's leg in 2006; looking at Rose during that time, one assumes he was too hungry to wait through the set.

VINCE NEIL

CHARGES: Vehicular manslaughter, DUI, battery, assault, domestic violence.

PUNISHMENT: Thirty total days in jail, $6.2 million and change in fines, fifteen days under house arrest.

Mötley Crüe frontman Vince Neil's crimes are especially heinous due to how little they harmed him. After killing Hanoi Rocks drummer Razzle in a drunk driving accident and causing brain damage to the occupants of the other car he hit, Neil only did fifteen days in jail; the hefty fine he paid mattered little to one of the richest rock stars in the world. Neil has never learned, and he has continued to get arrested for charges including assaulting a sex worker in Nevada.

VARG VIKERNES

CHARGES: Arson, murder.

PUNISHMENT: Twenty-one years in prison.

Frontman of the infamous one-man black-metal band Burzum, Varg "Count Grishnackh" Vikernes was part of Norway's original inner circle of church-burning black-metal terrorists. He stabbed his former mentor and Mayhem bandmate Øystein "Euronymous" Aarseth to death. The crime made international headlines, and resulted in Vikernes doing a paltry twenty-one years—the longest sentence available in Norway. He now makes idiotic racist YouTube screeds that appeal to Tolkien-loving shitbags. Look online for a very funny video of Immortal's Abbath mocking his prison sentence!

This asshole again?

Bard "Faust" Eithun of Emperor, back behind the kit after hard time, 2014.

BARD EITHUN

CHARGES: Murder.

PUNISHMENT: Nine years and four months in prison.

In an act of terrifying ruthlessness, Eithun agreed to follow a gay man out into the woods, stabbed him thirty-seven times, kicked him in the head, and then later bragged about it to his friends. In an interview, he described how he felt that meeting his victim was some kind of destiny. He was released from jail in 2003 after serving a little over half of his fourteen-year sentence. Norway, you may have noticed, does not do punishment very well.

TRIPP EISEN

CHARGES: Sexual assault of a minor.

PUNISHMENT: Seven months in prison.

Eisen was guitarist for industrial nu-metallers Static-X when he was arrested twice in one month for sexually assaulting an underage girl; the second time, he also kidnapped the victim. The band did the right thing and immediately ditched the guy, who went to prison from February to September 2005. Eisen has not released music since. Everyone's fine with that.

TIM LAMBESIS

CHARGES: Soliciting the murder of his wife.

PUNISHMENT: Six years in prison.

As I Lay Dying frontman Lambesis was 'roid'd the fuck out when he tried to hire someone from his gym to kill his wife and was caught when he met with an undercover agent posing as a hit man. His trial was ugly and obvious, with Lambesis appearing before the court a dejected muscle-bound wreck. He was found guilty and sentenced to six years in prison, during the course of which he attempted to sue two Southern California detention centers because coming off of his steroid regimen had caused him to grow breasts. No, really. As of September 2016, Lambesis is a free man, though still on parole.

Dream Theater annoys the crowd at the Chance in Poughkeepsie, New York, March 11, 1993.

A Crash Course in Prog Metal

Progressive metal draws heavily from progressive rock, in which highly skilled musicians write labyrinthine, technically complex songs to impress other musicians (see: Rush, King Crimson, etc.). Like prog rock, prog metal tends to focus lyrically on elaborate, fantastical, and allegorical narratives that are told over the entirety of one or more "concept albums." They're the kind of unabashedly nerdy bands that refer to their releases as "suites" and "movements." Beyond those basic tenets, however, the term "prog metal" is quite broad.

The most popular prog-metal band of all time is Dream Theater, which was started in 1985 by guitarist John Petrucci, drummer Mike Portnoy, and bassist John Myung when they were all students at the prestigious Berklee College of Music in Boston, Massachusetts. At its heaviest, the band is still pretty melodic; rhapsodic vocalist James LaBrie comes very much from the Ronnie James Dio school of singing; keyboard player Jordan Rudess looks like a wizard; its songs last longer than most lightbulbs; its drum kits could house the population of a small country; a woman has never willingly attended one of its concerts; and the level of musicianship on display is bonkers. Dream Theater's shows are probably about as close as metal gets to those of your average jam band (The Grateful Dead, Phish, etc.), punctuated by extended guitar, drum, keyboard, and six-string bass solos.

Québec's Voivod began as a thrash band before going prog with 1989's *Nothingface* (which even includes a cover of Pink Floyd's "Astronomy Domine"). The original material on the record blends a multitude of styles, including jazz, funk, psychedelic, and hardcore, into one otherworldly package. It seems likely that the band's members were influenced as much by the works of Dick and Ellison as they were any metal band, as their music, album art, and lyrics all have a sci-fi bent.

Queensrÿche, from Seattle, gained notice from MTV thanks to the ballad "Silent Lucidity," from 1990's *Empire*. But its most famous release is 1988's *Operation: Mindcrime*, a rock opera about a junkie-turned-revolutionary. It sounds like Halford fronting Dokken. Unfortunately, former vocalist Geoff Tate has become something of a punch line in metal

Violent lucidity: Queensrÿche wheedle on and fucking on, 1983.

thanks a massive ego and 2013's heinous *Frequency Unknown*, and young metal fans today may know the band best due to Tate's antics, not the group's music.

New Jersey's Symphony X is also melodic and synth-heavy. Lead vocalist Russell Allen sounds like Michael Bolton fronting a power-metal band, while the band's galloping rhythms owe a clear debt to thrash. The result has a gallant quality; if ever there was a metal soundtrack to a knight saving a princess from a dragon, it's the music of Symphony X.

Led by charismatic guitarist/vocalist Mikael Åkerfeldt, Opeth, from Stockholm, Sweden, was

one of the first bands to meld melodic death metal with prog rock. Albums such as *Orchid* (1995), *Blackwater Park* (2001), and *Ghost Reveries* (2005) are immense, lush, gothic howls of fury and anguish—the kind of metal Edgar Allen Poe might have appreciated. The band's keyboards usually sound like actual pianos or organs and not ray guns, and its guitars are bluesier than they are shreddy. On more recent releases like 2014's *Pale Communion* and 2016's *Sorceress*, the band has leaned into its love of psychedelic rock from the 1970s, with divisive results.

Canadian multi-instrumentalist and producer Devin Townsend first found fame singing for revered shredder Steve Vai on 1993's *Sex and Religion*, and later found success as the frontman for Strapping Young Lad (see Thrash Metal, 93). Along the way, the prolific Townsend has released nearly twenty solo albums that run the gamut of styles. Townsend's producing skills are also in high demand (he's recorded bands like Lamb of God and Darkest Hour), and he's one of the funniest live entertainers in metal.

Gojira, from Bayonne, France, makes Morbid Angel–esque deathgroove with lyrics about the environment and spirituality. Bandleaders Joe and Mario Duplantier are apotheosized for both their nimble musicianship and affable personalities.

Meanwhile, bands like Between the Buried and Me, from Raleigh, North Carolina, and Protest the Hero, from Ontario, Canada, have incorporated elements of metalcore into prog metal for the ADHD generation, often whipping the listener from one style to another with barely a segue provided for readjustment. These bands are, in a certain sense, the most progressive of all: they're less beholden to traditional songwriting structure or specific genre tropes than most of their forbearers. If that ain't progressive, nuthin' is.

"If you make one more King Crimson reference . . ." Opeth in London, November 2012.

Extra Credit

1. DREAM THEATER, "PULL ME UNDER"
(*Words and Images*, 1992)

2. OPETH, "GHOST OF PERDITION"
(*Ghost Reveries*, 2005)

3. DEVIN TOWNSEND, "SOLAR WINDS"
(*Ziltoid the Omniscient*, 2007)

4. BETWEEN THE BURIED AND ME, "FOAM BORN (A) THE BACKTRACK" AND "(B) THE DECADE OF STATUES"
(*Colors*, 2007)

5. GOJIRA, "OROBORUS"
(*The Way of All Flesh*, 2008)

10

Deathcore and Djent

WHAT IS IT?

Deathcore is basically metalcore, if metalcore bands loved hardcore and/or nu metal; djent is a poppier form of the off-kilter math metal of Sweden's Meshuggah.

WHO LISTENS TO IT?

Millennials.

WHERE DOES IT COME FROM?

The Internet.

BASTARD CHILDREN:

Sumeriancore.

THE BIG FOUR:

The Red Chord, Suicide Silence, Periphery, Animals as Leaders.

"Excuse my friends, ma'am. Some milk would be lovely." Suicide Silence, Extreme Thing Sport & Music Festival, Las Vegas, 2009.

metalcore effectively erased the line between metal and hardcore, accepting a very broad definition of "metal." Whereas in the past thrash fans and glam fans wanted to kick each other's asses almost as much as metal fans and hardcore fans, the metalcore generation's attitude was ostensibly, "If it feels good, we're playing it." This mentality extended to the next generation of metal bands as well.

Mark Heylmun is the lead guitarist for one of the most popular deathcore acts of all time: Suicide Silence, from California's Inland Empire. He remembers auditioning for the band in 2005, before he'd even turned eighteen. The group's members asked him who his influences were, and he assumed he had to emphasize the heaviest bands possible. "At the time, I wasn't really a death metal guy," he recalls. "I was much more into Metallica, Pantera, classic rock, Sabbath, Maiden, Ozzy, Zeppelin, shit like that." But Heylmun was concerned those artists lacked the proper cred. "So I remember citing the death metal that I liked . . . 'I like Cattle Decapitation! And I saw Suffocation and Crytopsy with them. And I saw Dying Fetus with GWAR!'"

To Heylmun's surprise, that actually wasn't the response the others wanted. "They're like, 'Yeah, but what else do you like? Do you just listen to death metal?' And they start talking about what they're into—'My favorite band's Korn,' 'I like System of a Down.' And I thought it was badass that everyone was admitting to liking these bands that are not so cool to admit to liking when you're involved in a brutal or hardcore scene."

That, in a nutshell, is deathcore at its purest: genre-bending death metal as made by dudes who give zero fucks about being perceived as "true." Heylmun even credits this perceived divide as being responsible for the term 'deathcore.'

> **I think the first time I ever heard [the term "deathcore"] was when we were joking around in our own practice spot about it. Because it was kinda weird having patch-wearers and "true" death metal dudes not like our music because of breakdowns . . . they'd be at the shows, but they'd literally stand there with their arms crossed, shouting, "You suck!"**

> **So we were joking around in the band room, saying, we could call it "deathcore" or "hardcore death metal."**

The Acacia Strain smelling themselves, April 2006.

"THIS IS HOW I EAT A HOT DOG!" The Red Chord, August 4, 2006.

"WHERE WE'RE GOING, WE DON'T NEED ROADS"

Perhaps no band better exemplifies deathcore's no-shits-given attitude than the Red Chord. One simply needed to look at these dudes from Revere, Massachusetts, to immediately comprehend that they were not your father's death metal band. Charismatic vocalist Guy Kozowyk later went on to become a cop; he and his bandmates did not look like guys who played under a moniker that is a euphemism for a slit throat. No sleeve tats or inverted crosses burned into faces here; at worst,

guitarist Mike "Gunface" McKenzie and bassist Greg Weeks sometimes sported large beards, but even then, they basically just looked like hip dads from Brooklyn.

Furthermore, the band dared to demonstrate a sense of humor, giving songs titles like "Jar Full of Bunny Parts" and fast becoming specialists in fucking with both members of younger bands (as in two now-notorious video interviews for the website *Metal Injection*) as well as its own fans. For example, Kozowyk would sometimes begin shows by declaring, "All right, this is your last chance to dance!"—a phrase traditionally used by metal bands to announce the final song. The band also helped begin a now long-held deathcore tradition of releasing shirts in bright colors, the likes of which have been previously off-limits in the metal world.

Its music, of course, is where the Red Chord really differentiated itself from your run-of-the-mill Deicide wannabes. Its 2002 debut album, appropriately entitled *Fused Together in Revolving Doors*, was an epileptic amalgamation of tech-death, grindcore, hardcore, doom metal, and sheer weirdness (signature song "Dreaming in Dog Years" includes the use of a stock beat from a cheap, Casio-like keyboard). Traditional verse/chorus/verse song structures were not invited to this party. Anytime the listener thinks he or she has a handle on a particular section of any given song, the riff changes suddenly and without warning. The Red Chord simply did not believe in rules.

The band truly hit its stride with its second effort, 2005's *Clients*. Its members didn't change their style very much from *Fused Together in Revolving Doors*, but they did perfect it. The abrupt stylistic shifts felt more organic, McKenzie's riffs more nimble and dizzying. Kozowyk also stepped up his game in a big way. Each track on *Clients* is told from the point of view of a different person with a different mental illness, which allowed him to write lyrics that were creative, funny, and disturbing all at once, as on "Upper Decker," where Kozowyk advises the listener to "shit your pants and run for your life" before inexplicably wondering, "Whose toast is this?"

Kozowyk's new approach to writing lyrics not only better suited the Red Chord's singular style of music, it also better reflected the existential and psychological fears of the new generation of death-metal fans, who were raised not on slasher films but on meds administered by helicopter parents on different meds.

Clients avoided the dreaded "sophomore slump," landing the band a coveted spot on Ozzfest and becoming the first album to ever receive a perfect score in its *Decibel* review. Unfortunately, the band's third album, 2007's *Prey for Eyes*, was not as well received. Some fans complained that the record was simply too straightforward, without enough of the oddities that made *Fused Together* and *Clients* so memorable. The group was able to right the ship creatively with its next release, 2009's *Fed Through the Teeth Machine*, but from a commercial standpoint, the band never quite recovered. Save for the occasional show or mini-tour, its members remained relatively quiet in recent years. Time will tell if some version of the Red Chord will ever make another record.

Despised Icon in Sheffield, England, on the Never Say Die tour, in 2009, pictured yelling, "DIE!"

GILES COREY'S LAST WORDS

Besides the Red Chord, there are three other groups who are generally credited with being the first deathcore bands: the Acacia Strain, also from Massachusetts; and Despised Icon and Ion Dissonance, both from Montréal, Québec. Ion Dissonance had a heavy mathcore influence, interweaving angular guitar noodling with lots of chunky low-end played in discombobulating rhythms. The Acacia Strain and Despised Icon, meanwhile, basically made death metal in the style of hardcore, offering massive, simple riffs played in the lowest possible tuning, foot-breaking double-bass drums, breakdowns, gang shouts, and, in Despised Icon's case, a style of vocals that became known as "pig squeals" because it sounded like Ned Beatty making sweet redneck love in the movie *Deliverance*.

While the Red Chord are the most well-respected by metal's elite, Despised Icon and the Acacia Strain were ultimately the most influential to the deathcore acts that followed. Part of this is almost certainly because their sound was easier to duplicate, but part of it may also have been due to the bands' images: the Acacia Strain's hilariously goofy frontman, Vincent Bennett, and Despised Icon co-vocalists Steve Marois and Alex Erian all wore straight-brim baseball caps and basketball jerseys, which made them look more like stereotypical Eminem fans than stereotypical Entombed fans, but they also had throat tats and massive gauges (circular piercings that stretch the earlobe out to an uncomfortable degree). To a generation of kids whose gateway into extreme music was bands that often mixed uncomplicated rock riffs with hip-hop aesthetics (see Nu Metal, page 207), the Acacia Strain and Despised Icon hit the sweet spot of "similar-yet-different."

Thus the stage was almost set for those Korn-loving kids in Suicide Silence to truly set the deathcore trend . . .

Almost.

TELL SUPERMAN HE CAN STAY HOME

In 2005, Job for a Cowboy, from Glendale, Arizona, self-released *Doom* while its members were still in high school. The six-song EP was massively popular, despite the group being unsigned, unmanaged, and unable to drink legally. The reason? Its expert use of a then-new online social platform, MySpace. The band amassed so many Internet followers that the industry was forced to take notice, and, in 2006, JFAC signed with Metal Blade Records.

Death-metal purists promptly decided that JFAC sucked.

This opinion was purely superficial, based mostly on the band's arch name, a hatred of vocalist Jonny Davy's pig squeals, and a perception that its online road to success somehow represented the death of heavy metal and not the dawn of a new era in sharing art. Had these homunculi actually listened to *Doom*, they'd have noted that it's an above-average Dying Fetus duplication. And had they shown up for the rest of JFAC's discography, they would have noticed a complete absence of pig squeals alongside an ever-increasing emphasis on musicianship, wholly devoid of any "core" elements.

Doom was made by kids. Kids, generally speaking, have no idea what the fuck they want to do with themselves, and, as a rule, they get better at shit as they get older ("practice makes perfect" and all that). This being the case, the band kept undergoing lineup changes, with Davy its only consistent member. Davy, in turn, kept pushing the music in a non-core direction while recruiting increasingly talented musicians, such as drummer John "Charn" Rice, guitarists Tony Sannicandro and Al Glassman, and bassist Nick Schendzielos, to fill out the lineup. The result: two flat-out masterpieces of progressive tech-death, *Demonocracy* (2012) and *Sun Eater* (2014).

But the purists didn't give those albums a chance, and the kids who had loved the pig-squealing version of the band didn't appreciate the music's new direction. And so Job for a Cowboy's popularity was fleeting . . . whereas Suicide Silence, hot on its heels, flourished.

Despised Icon, recently shorn for their wool, at Irving Plaza in New York City, August 11, 2009.

THE SOUND OF SILENCE

Now Suicide Silence—here was a band that was fuckin' deathcore right down to the bone. Case in point: ask Mark Heylmun to define "deathcore," and he replies with a chuckle, "Everything that Suicide Silence does musically is going to be called 'deathcore.' There's just no way around it."

The band's self-titled EP, released in 2005, is a churning, diseased, sixteen-minute explosion of oppressive savagery that sounds as though someone took Cannibal Corpse and edited out what little nuance it had. The group quickly gained a local following, which included Heylmun, who remembers being especially impressed by the band's lanky, heavily tattooed frontman, Mitch Lucker:

> **Mitch was a fucking force. I'd never really seen anybody do what he was doing the way he was doing it, so confidently. And then, after the set, I'd always see him in the pit. . . . I admit, I was afraid of the guy at first. I was like, "This dude is fucking insane."**

Century Media soon signed the band, releasing its full-length debut, *The Cleansing*, in 2007. The album is music's answer to repeatedly getting punched in the head by Deontay Wilder. It sounds like someone has turned Morbid Angel upside-down and started shaking its members for hidden money.

Detractors claimed that the band sounded too much like death-metal vocals over tuned-down Korn—without realizing that was kind of the point. *The Cleansing* was the first death-metal album for the nu-metal generation. Fans flocked to it like flies to a corpse. Suicide Silence's follow-up, 2009's *No Time to Bleed*, debuted at #32 on the Billboard 200, selling a cool fourteen thousand copies in its first week of release. In 2011, its third album, *The Black Crown*, charted even higher, coming in at #28.

But tragedy struck on November 1, 2012, when Lucker was killed as the result of injuries sustained in a motorcycle accident. He was just twenty-eight years old, and he left behind a wife, Jolie Carmadella, and a five-year-old daughter, Kenadee. At a candlelight vigil held days after his death, Carmadella claimed that Lucker was drunk at the time of his accident: "I tried to stop him. I was in front of him begging him not to leave the house. Begging him. Like, 'Just seriously, for us, don't leave.' And he did. And this is what happened."

Naturally, there was some initial doubt as to whether or not Suicide Silence could, would, or should continue with a new singer. But following a show to benefit Kenadee, during which the band performed with a rotating cast of notable deathcore vocalists, the remaining members recruited Hernan "Eddie" Hermida to step into Lucker's very large shoes. Hermida was a smart choice: not only was he every bit the instigator a good metal frontman needs to be, he arrived with his own cred, having just spent a decade in another popular, somewhat more traditionally deathy deathcore band, All Shall Perish. In 2014, Suicide Silence released its first album with Hermida, *You Can't Stop Me*, to an overwhelmingly positive response: it sold fifteen thousand copies in its first week of release, landing it at #16 on the Billboard 200.

DEATHBORE

That same year, Whitechapel, from Knoxville, Tennessee, released its fifth album, *Our Endless War*. It debuted at #10 on the Billboard 200, selling more than sixteen thousand copies right out of the gate. It was now readily apparent that deathcore wasn't going anywhere, regardless of what the old guard made of it.

Which isn't to say that deathcore hasn't birthed a lot of shit bands. You can recognize these groups from a mile away, because they're more famous for their antics than their music. Emmure, from Queens, is fronted by Frankie Palmeri, a Limp Bizkit–loving conspiracy theorist whose intellectual, aesthetic, and moral offenses could fill their own book. Winds of Plague, from San Bernardino, California, holds the unique honor of being the metal band with the most members to have had nude photos wind up on revenge porn sites (three and counting). Oceano, from Chicago, has certainly mastered the art of monotony. More recently, Australia's Thy Art is Murder

have become be wildly popular—offering proof of Slayer's theory about how a higher power feels about us mortals.

What these "deathbore" bands have in common is a performance art–like devotion to aural plateaus. A popular online video demonstrates how to play an Emmure-esque atonal two-note guitar breakdown with a single string. The band uses sub-oceanic tunings and seven-string guitars to make sure it sounds like a wrecking ball, but produce endless, generic non-riffs for its endless, generic non-songs. If you've ever wanted to know what it would feel like to have a migraine while stuck in a coma, these are the bands for you.

At least partially to repudiate these bands, in 2017 Suicide Silence released a self-titled album featuring an abundance of clean vocals and a paucity of material that sounded like traditional deathcore. Following an online uproar, the record sold only 4,650 copies in its initial week—barely a third of the first-week sales figures for *You Can't Stop Me*. When it comes to commercialism, it's apparently better to be brain-dead than to take a creative risk.

Frankie Palimeri of Emmure watching God flip him off at the Corporation in Sheffield, England, November 12, 2009.

BUT DOES IT DJENT?

Meanwhile, despite the best efforts of the anti-JFAC set, the Internet continued to be a thing. And while old fuddy-duddies wrote think pieces about how the net could potentially destroy the very notion of a "regional sound," younger fans understood how to get the most out of the web: by using it as a tool for learning in between time spent on hardcore pornography and kitten photos.

Enter Misha Mansoor. A native of Bethesda, Maryland, he got his first guitar for his bar mitzvah in 1997, and was already a metal fan when he was given a destiny-altering recommendation a few years later.

"Someone was like, 'Oh, you like Slipknot and Dream Theater? You should check out this band Meshuggah,'" he recalls. "And I checked out some stuff off of *Chaosphere*, and I was like, 'This is garbage, it's random and it's just noise and I hate it.'"

Then a jazz bassist friend got Mansoor to reconsider.

He said, "Oh they're that band that always plays in 4/4." And I was like, "No, you must be thinking of a different band," and he was like, "No, that's their deal, it doesn't sound like they're playing in 4/4 but literally everything they play is in 4/4."

So then I re-listened to it, and I realized I was listening to the music all wrong, and suddenly I thought, "Oh my god, this is the most genius band." That was a moment in my life that changed pretty much everything.

Not long after that, Mansoor remembers, "I started writing music and making music on my computer and realizing I could do that." Then he started sharing that music, often under the moniker "Bulb," on the message boards for Meshuggah, Dream Theater guitar god John Petrucci, and several forums dedicated to gear.

I didn't really know a lot of people in real life who were into the kind of music I was into. Remember, back then, nobody was really listening to this kind of music, the kind of stuff I was doing was not cool to most people. So it was kind of a community where people were actually embracing these demos I was posting up, which encouraged me to keep posting there.

"Dude." "Dude." "DUDE." Periphery's Mark Holcomb (left) and Misha Mansoor (right), The Fillmore in San Francisco, California, August 14, 2016.

Although it took him some time to find other young players who were able to emulate Messugah's unusual approach to music, eventually, Mansoor was able to put together a band, Periphery.

Periphery wasn't the first young band to borrow heavily from Meshuggah; as Mansoor himself notes, England's SikTh and the Netherlands' Textures "were doing it way before anyone," and the Philadelphia band A Life Once Lost certainly channeled the Swedes on early albums like *A Great Artist* (2003). But much like Refused and Darkest Hour before them, they were just a little too far ahead of their time, and didn't quite "catch on" the way they deserved to. And so, as Mansoor and Periphery's fame continued to spread across the net, they became the ones to actually popularize the Meshuggah sound.

This sound has come to be known as "djent"—which, Mansoor explains, is actually a misuse of the word:

Fredrik [Thordendal, Meshuggah guitarist] coined the term to describe their guitar tone. Because they played their power chords a little differently than how most people do it. Power chords are usually played with two or three strings, and using four strings gives you that extra metallic tone to it. And they would palm mute aggressively. And that was their chosen onomatopoeia for the sound—"djent." It's a signature of their sound, something I totally ripped off from them, as did every other band subsequently.

Above: Whitechapel's Phil Bozeman rallies fans in a singalong about vivisection in Sheffield, England, November 5, 2010. Below: Animals as Leaders nod simultaneously to remember the kick-in point in Bristol, England, November 9, 2014.

Sometime between Periphery's first two releases, *Periphery* (2010) and *Periphery II: This Time It's Personal* (2012), two things happened. First, Periphery's lineup—which now included drummer Matt Halpern, guitarists Jake Bowen and Mark Holcomb, vocalist Spencer Sotelo, and bassist Adam "Nolly" Getgood—solidified. Second, "djent" came to denote an entire subgenre of metal, which also included bands populated by Mansoor's friends from his message-board days, like guitarists Alec "Acle" Kahney (TesseracT) and John Browne (Monuments). All of these bands owed a substantial debt to Meshuggah, but like those from the worlds of metalcore and deathcore, they weren't afraid to incorporate other influences into their music, such as metalcore's good cop/bad cop vocals and breakdowns, nu- and hair metal's talents for pop songwriting, Pantera's cavernous groove (see A Crash Course in Groove Metal and Sludge, page 172), and Nevermore's awesomely dorky prog metal. (Nevermore lead guitarist Jeff Loomis provides a guest solo on *Periphery*'s closing track, the fifteen-minute "Racecar.") Thus, djent bands were able to make old tricks seem new again.

Fans responded in a big way, and djent spawned its own subgenre in record time: bands like Born of Osiris, Veil of Maya, and After the Burial were dubbed "Sumeriancore" on account of all sounding similar and all being early signings to Sumerian Records (as was Periphery). These groups amalgamated djent with deathcore, creating something heavier than Periphery but more forgiving than the Acacia Strain.

The members of Periphery, meanwhile, became icons within the musician community. Mansoor is especially revered, and understandably so. His success story is truly unique to the twenty-first

century: the idea of a kid being able to record and release great-sounding music on his computer would simply not have been possible ten years earlier. It's only natural that so many should attempt to follow in his footsteps, or, in some cases, do him one better: Cloudkicker, for example, is actually a one-man band, written, recorded, produced, and distributed by multi-instrumentalist Ben Sharp, who has foregone labels and managers altogether.

Although doubters tried to dismiss Mansoor as a so-called "bedroom producer," it wasn't long before he was recording not just his own music but that of other bands, too . . . most notably, Animals as Leaders, an instrumental trio from Washington, D.C.

The project was created by guitarist Tosin Abasi, who got his start in a metalcore band called Reflux (which also included future Sumerian Records founder Ash Avildsen); when Reflux broke up, E. J. Johantgen, co-founder of Prosthetic Records, set about talking Abasi into recording a solo album. After a year of studying music, Abasi took Johantgen up on his offer. Abasi self-recorded all his own guitar and bass tracks; Mansoor then stepped in to record some additional guitar solos, program the drums, and mix the record.

The result, 2009's *Animals as Leaders*, was both a forward-thinking declaration of arrival and a throwback to old Shrapnel Records instrumental releases by virtuosos like Jason Becker and Paul Gilbert. It made Abasi a guitar hero virtually overnight, and understandably so. Abasi is a showman who shreds seven- and eight-string guitars with two-handed tapping and slapping and sweep picking and every other flashy trick in the book, but he also utilizes jazz theory and classical guitar and electronica-style bleeps and bloops.

As a genius, a genre-busting musician, and a dapperly dressed African American, Abasi may also be the greatest personification of all the ways in which metal has changed since its inception. It's no longer mandatory for a metal fan to look like one of the thugs who becomes fodder for Charles Bronson in a *Death Wish* movie, no longer mandatory to refuse the allowance of other genres into your musical diet, no longer mandatory for metal to be made by Caucasian heterosexual men for other Caucasian heterosexual men, and no longer mandatory, in fact, to do anything other than to raise hell.

As we said in our introduction: now, more than ever, metal is for everyone.

Starter Kit

Ready to open yours arms
to damnation? You will need:

☐ TO HAVE BEEN BORN NO EARLIER THAN 1980

☐ DEATHCORE LOGO BASKETBALL SHORTS

☐ V-NECK T-SHIRT, WHITE

☐ EAR GAUGES (OPTIONAL BUT ENCOURAGED)

☐ ONE (1) GUITAR WITH NO FEWER THAN SEVEN (7) STRINGS

☐ ZERO (0) POSSESSION OF ANY PHYSICAL MEDIA (CDS, VINYL, ETC.)

☐ ONE (1) HOME RECORDING STUDIO (AUTHENTIC DRUMS OPTIONAL)

☐ ONE (1) ACCOUNT ON EVERY POPULAR ONLINE SOCIAL PLATFORM, INCLUDING, BUT NOT LIMITED TO, FACEBOOK, TWITTER, INSTAGRAM, SNAPCHAT, REDDIT, AND TINDER

☐ A VERY THICK SKIN

☐ NO LESS THAN A 75 PERCENT CHANCE THAT THERE'S A NUDE PHOTOGRAPH OF YOU ON THE INTERNET SOMEWHERE

Homework

1. THE RED CHORD, "BLACK SANTA"

(Clients, 2005)

2. ION DISSONANCE, "THE SURGE"

(Minus the Herd, 2007)

3. DESPISED ICON, "A FRACTURED HAND"

(The Ills of Modern Man, 2007)

4. THE ACACIA STRAIN, "JONESTOWN"

(Wormwood, 2010)

5. THE TONY DANZA TAPDANCE EXTRAVAGANZA, "THE LOST AND DAMNED"

(Danza 3: The Series of Unfortunate Events, 2010)

6. WHITECHAPEL, "THE SAW IS THE LAW"

(Our Endless War, 2014)

7. JOB FOR A COWBOY, "ENTOMBMENT OF A MACHINE"

(Doom, 2005)

8. JOB FOR A COWBOY, "THE DEITY MISCONCEPTION"

(Demonocracy, 2012)

9. SUICIDE SILENCE, "UNANSWERED"

(The Cleansing, 2008)

10. ALL SHALL PERISH, "ERADICATION"

(The Price of Existence, 2006)

11. SIKTH, "SANGUINE SEAS OF BIGOTRY"

(Death of a Dead Day, 2006)

12. PERIPHERY, "RAGNAROK"

(Periphery II, 2012)

13. ANIMALS AS LEADERS, "CAFO"

(Animals as Leaders, 2009)

14. TEXTURES, "SANGUINE DRAWS THE OATH"

(Dualism, 2011)

15. CHIMSPANNER, "SUPEREROGATION"

(At the Dream's Edge, 2010)

16. TESSERACT, "CONCEALING FATE PART ONE—ACCEPTANCE"

(Concealing Fate, 2010)

17. CLOUDKICKER, "WE'RE GOIN' IN. WE'RE GOING DOWN."

(Beacons, 2009)

18. THE CONTORTIONIST, "HOLOMOVEMENT"

(Intrinsic, 2012)

19. BORN OF OSIRIS, "OPEN ARMS TO DAMNATION"

(The New Reign, 2007)

20. VEIL OF MAYA, "NAMASTE"

(—id—, 2010)

21. AFTER THE BURIAL, "YOUR TROUBLES WILL CEASE AND FORTUNE WILL SMILE UPON YOU"

(In Dreams, 2010)

Index

Photo Credits

Acknowledgments

The authors would like to thank
(and in no fucking way is this in order of priority):

FOR THEIR INTERVIEWS: Frank Bello, Alex Webster, Paul Mazurkiewicz, Jesse Leach, Misha Mansoor, Otep Shamaya, Mark Heylmun, Hunter Hunt-Hendrix, Eyal Levi, Mirai Kawashima, Dez Fafara, Rob Cavestany, Ted Aguilar, Ben Hutcherson, and Scott Weinrich.

FOR THEIR HELP: Frank Godla, Kim Kelly, Ben Burstein, Lily Domash, Vince Edwards, Denise Santoro, Heidi Robinson-Fitzgerald, Liz Ciavarella-Brenner, Charles Elliot, Paul Schlessinger, Julie Arkenstone, Amy Sciaretto, George Vallee, Monica Seide-Evenson, Jon Freeman, Sammi Chichester, and everyone at *Revolver*.

FOR THEIR HARD WORK: Jeannine Dillon, Phil Buchanan, Jon Chaiet, and the inimitable Mark Riddick.

FOR THEIR ENABLEMENT: Dave Castillo and everyone at Saint Vitus Bar, Jimmy Duff and everyone at Duff's Brooklyn, Melody and everyone at Lucky 13, Nick Nunns and the Trve Brewing crew.

FOR THEIR LOYALTY, SUPPORT, AND LOVE: Jan and Sydney Goldenberg, Ben "Vince Neilstein" Umanov and Emily Mitchell-Marell and Maximus Umanov, Azara Golston, Anna Quindlen, Gerry Krovatin, Maria Krovatin, Quin Krovatin, Lynn Feng, Arthur Krovatin, Alex Wenner, Zach Smith, Rob Pasbani, Lawrence Derks, Natalya Matushkina, Michael and Janie and Ida Slavens, Greg and Sarah Marcy, Evan Berger and Michelle Feldman, Eduardo Wong and Claudia Davila, Sido Abbene and Shane Abess and Tyrion and Océane Abbene-Abess, Justin Foley, Bob Lugowe, Marla Haut, Ken Lee and Candice Alustiza-Lee, David Brodsky and Allison Woest, Bram Teitelman, Steve Joh, Monte Conner, Anso DF, Nick Emde, Ben Apatoff, Liz Snair, Luis Alvarenga, Morgan "Bloodbath" McGrath, Brandon and Maya Geist, Doug Moore, Caroline Harrison, Wyatt Marshall, Nate Garrett, Zack Rose, Lauren Grace, Sarah Marafi, Joseph Olehnik, Sam Turner, Max Baehr and Abbie Walker, James McBride, and that loveable fucker Brian Storm.

NO THANKS AND FUCK OFF TO: Anyone who thinks metal is a home for racism, sexism, homophobia, or other forms of bigotry; people who casually use slurs against minorities as an insult; self-proclaimed anti-PC warriors; Phil Labonte, who's all three of the previous things; heroin; all major religious institutions; the bus that crushed Cliff Burton; that guy who sold Chris a fake Henry Rollins ticket in 2005; Michael Berberian; Don Blood; that one band from Australia (you know who are); the state of New Jersey; and, of course, Nathan Gale. Nathan, we hope there's a Hell, just for you.